FACT-BASED BRANDING
IN THE REAL WORLD

A Simple Survival Guide
for CMOs and Brand Managers

FACT-BASED BRANDING IN THE REAL WORLD

Rolf M. Wulfsberg, PhD
rwulfsberg@siegelgale.com

ISBN: 978-0-9885555-0-1

Printed in the United States of America

Additional Praise for Fact-Based Branding in the Real World: A Simple Survival Guide for CMOs and Brand Managers

"I have enormous respect for Dr. Wulfsberg's professionalism, passion, and reliability. He has been an invaluable resource for me the past 6 years with his extraordinary ability to design research that measures the effectiveness of strategies and messages generating the desired supporting behavior— what I call the "so what" factor. His focus on providing actionable research is refreshing."

Alan Siegel, Founder and Chairman Emeritus of Siegel+Gale and President and CEO of Siegelvision

"Branding without sound and actionable intelligence is a black art, not a science. Dr. Wulfsberg continues to pioneer new ways to get to the "compelling truth" at the heart of any great brand. Read and learn!"

Scott Lerman, Founder and CEO, Lucid Brands

"This book should be on everyone's shelf either to remind you of branding research core principles or ground you on why fact-based decision making is a must for the branding journey. Branding can feel elusive, but it shouldn't if you've done your homework. This is the homework guide so your decisions are grounded. Simple, Elegant, Excellent."

Lisa Fawcett, Vice President, Global Marketing, CooperVision

"Dr. Wulfsberg's '10 Reasons to Embrace Fact-Based Branding' are spot on. Nothing could have aligned our senior leadership more than the concrete data derived using the principles outlined in this book. Brands can elicit very emotional behaviors from even the most seasoned executives. By removing the subjective, emotional aspects from the equation and focusing on the market facts, our team easily agreed on a single direction for our brand."

Kathleen Hertzog, Vice President, Marketing & Communications, Availity

"Today's savvy CMOs and brand managers rely on brand research to help craft positioning and guide marketing investments. But what happens if that brand research is flawed? In this very readable volume, Dr. Wulfsberg provides just

the information that CMOs need to become better buyers and users of brand research, and ultimately gain ground on competitors. Spend an hour or two with Rolf's book and apply one or two of his ideas. You'll be glad you did."

Dr. James C. Fink, President, Analytics, Infinia Group

"Over the past several years we have built the beginnings of a robust research program. After reading his book, I know now that we've just been skimming the surface. There are so many more ways in which we can gauge the efficacy of our marketing and grow our brand."

Zari Talebi, Senior Manager, Global Brand and Integrated Communications, Eaton Corporation

Table of Contents

Foreword

I've been a practicing statistician for 43 years, initially with the federal government and then in the business world, where I specialize in brand research and customer satisfaction research. My doctorate is in mathematical statistics, yet while that training gave me an excellent foundation in statistics, it didn't prepare me for the real world. Academic training presents statistical methods that apply under a set of prescribed conditions, but in the real world, the data you are analyzing seldom meet these basic assumptions. In the real world, missing data is the rule rather than the exception, and you have to come up with pragmatic solutions on a regular basis. My objective in writing this book was to pass on many of the lessons I've learned over the years that were not taught in graduate school—and still aren't.

For many Chief Marketing Officers (CMOs) and brand managers, statistical analysis may sound complex and intimidating. While it's true that you do have to know a few things to use it properly, the very purpose of market research and statistical analysis is to cut through complexity and confusion and get to the heart of what really matters. While some statistical tools are fairly complicated—simple doesn't mean simplistic—the intent of this book is to make market research and fact-based branding in the real world as simple as possible to understand and embrace and use in your business.

I originally wrote the manuscript for this book nearly two years ago. At that point, it was little more than a loose collection of many of the things I had learned during my career, and it lacked structure and organization (not to mention an audience). I put the book aside, hoping to get back to it before it was too late. Recently, however, I found the impetus I needed.

A client of mine asked me to rewrite a report she had received from a research firm in Taiwan. Upon reading the report, I became very upset. I could forgive the authors for their many misunderstandings of the English language (which made the report almost unreadable), but their research methodology was unacceptable. They had included survey results from respondents who acknowledged having no role whatsoever in the purchasing decision and who had no relation to the category under consideration. On top of that, the researchers included ratings on brands the respondents said they had never heard of. In short, the report was irresponsible and complete unusable.

Fortunately my client was savvy enough to recognize that things were not right with the research. But what if she hadn't been? What actions might she have taken based on such faulty research? The people who prepared that report are fellow researchers—my professional colleagues. This kind of malfeasance gives my profession a bad name among those it is intended to support. And worse, research poorly executed can actually do more damage and be more misleading than no research at all. This experience renewed my determination to complete this book and get it into the field, where it might do some good. The marriage of brand research and brand strategy has been truly rewarding to me, and I felt it was time for me to give back to these great fields.

I rewrote the book in two volumes, for two distinct audiences. *Fact-Based Branding in the Real World: A Simple Survival Guide for CMOs and Brand Managers* is aimed at those who build and manage brands, and my goal is to inspire them to embrace fact-based branding and get the most out of it. *Fact-Based Branding in the Real World: A Simple Survival Guide for Research Professionals* (to be released soon) is geared toward research professionals, either inside client companies or in research firms that support client companies. This second volume aims to reveal many of the on-the-job lessons I've learned over the past 43 years, in the hope that the reader can avoid repeating those mistakes at their clients' expense. I want to see the quality of the research from these professionals improve.

The two books are very similar—a few of the chapters are identical—except that *Fact-Based Branding in the Real World: A Simple Survival Guide for Research Professionals* includes levels of mathematical and statistical detail (complete with Greek letters and subscripts) that few CMOs would either tolerate or enjoy. The objective of creating these two parallel volumes is to foster discussions between brand and marketing executives and the brand researchers who support them, so that both sides can work together and build stronger brands.

Over the last four decades, I've had the good fortune to work for some great research and consulting firms, and to learn from true gurus in the field, such as Dr. Frederick Mosteller of Harvard University, Dr. John Tukey of Princeton University and AT&T Bell Laboratories, and Rory Morgan at Research International. On the brand strategy side, I learned a tremendous amount from leaders such as Jim Johnson and Scott Lerman while I was at Enterprise IG (now The Brand Union) and the legendary Alan Siegel at Siegel+Gale. Finally, I've had the honor and pleasure of working for remarkable leaders of industry as clients, such as Hugh McColl at NationsBank and Bank of America and Dick Cheney when he was CEO of Halliburton.

I want to express my gratitude to Dr. Michele Davis-Collins and Brian Rafferty, who worked with me tirelessly in developing some of the ideas and solutions to difficult real-world problems we encountered. Deep thanks as well to Irene Etzkorn, Dawn O'Polka, Zari Talebi and Scott Lerman for reviewing my manuscript and offering invaluable suggestions. Thanks to Jeff Garigliano who edited the book, Matthias Mencke who designed the cover and layout, serial comma killer Claire de Brunner for her eagle-eyed proof-reading and Gail Zuniga for the great information graphics. You all work magic. And finally, the publication of this book would not have been possible without the support of Siegel+Gale co-CEOs Howard Belk and David Srere and CMO Gail Nelson.

This book is dedicated to my daughter, Dr. Anne-Marie Johnson and my son, Paul Montello. Anna, as you independently chose to work in the research field, I hope this book offers some ideas and thoughts that will make your work easier.

Fundamentals of fact-based branding

This section explains what fact-based branding means and how it can simplify your life as a CMO or brand manager.

Read this section when you are reviewing your brand's research plan to ensure that the research will help you understand how decision makers select one brand over another across the entire customer life cycle. In addition, read this section before you approve a specific research questionnaire to ensure it's sound.

Chapter 1
What Is Fact-Based Branding?

If you're a CMO or brand manager, we can reasonably assume that your company recognizes the concept of branding. But how does the company develop its brand strategy? How does it measure the effectiveness of brand initiatives? (Or does it measure this at all?)

Typically, companies develop brand strategies for their overall corporate identity and their products and services using one of three approaches:

+ The dictate of management
+ The judgment of brand gurus
+ Facts derived from research

The principal difference among these three is the amount of "due diligence" they involve. In the first case, branding by management fiat, the CEO or some other executive simply dictates the brand's positioning and strategy. While some major firms have used this approach successfully for much of their existence—Bloomberg didn't even have a CMO until a few years ago—most now base their brand decisions on additional factors.

The second approach, judgment-based branding, relies on the intuitive abilities of people like CMOs, brand managers and branding consultants to understand how people buy products and services and what types of messages will influence those buyers. This isn't to suggest that CEOs who dictate a strategy don't use judgment; rather, judgment-based branding simply allows more room for discussion and disagreement.

In fact, the real roots of brand consulting are in judgment-based branding. The brand consulting business began in the mid-20th century with firms such as Lippincott & Margulies, Siegel+Gale, Landor and Diefenbach Elkins (now Future-Brand). For decades, these firms focused on building corporate and brand identities for clients, primarily by designing impressive logos and attractive business cards and annual reports.

Would you acquire another company without a pro forma balance sheet and significant additional due diligence? Would you construct an office building without a blueprint? Of course not. Then why would you base the positioning and strategy of one of your most valuable assets on a lesser degree of due diligence?

During this period, which lasted until roughly the turn of the 21st century, any forays into brand strategy were largely qualitative in nature, relying heavily on the expertise of senior brand consultants. A typical brand strategy assignment included a handful of interviews with executives inside the client company, along with external customers and prospects. The brand consultants might have thrown in a few focus groups and some audits of collateral materials for good measure. This is a small amount of information, but the business model relied on "gurus" who could extrapolate from the information and develop brand strategy recommendations.

Judgment-based branding is very much alive and well today, on both the consulting side and the client side. It's particularly prevalent among companies that don't believe that branding is a legitimate science, or that investments in rigorous brand research will pay off.

Despite those perceptions—or misperceptions—many companies have evolved beyond this point and now use the third and most concrete approach: fact-based branding. Because this is such a crucial concept, it's worth an explicit definition.

By "fact-based branding," I mean the use of rigorous quantitative measurement and forecasting techniques to make better branding decisions. Fact-based branding covers the entire customer life cycle—from the acquisition of new customers to the retention and expansion of existing customer relationships. For that reason, I include customer satisfaction research.

Fact-based branding has grown in popularity in recent years, as companies have increasingly realized that their corporate brand and major product and/or service brands are among the most valuable assets they own. Accordingly, decisions affecting those brands deserve a commensurate degree of due diligence. This is particularly the case in industries where performance is driven by numbers—like banking, insurance, telecommunications and engineering, among others. Companies that have adopted Six Sigma principles are also more likely to embrace fact-based branding.

Think of it this way. Would you acquire another company without poring through its financials and constructing a pro forma balance sheet? Would you construct an office building without a blueprint? Of course not. Then why would you entrust the positioning and strategy of one of your most valuable assets to a lesser degree of due diligence?

IBM's 2011 Global Chief Marketing Officer Study suggests that 80 percent of CMOs now rely on market research and competitive benchmarking to make strategic decisions. But how many of those CMOs truly understand the research they are being provided? Are they certain that the research and the professionals providing the information are absolutely top-notch? Are they getting everything out of the research that they could?

According to Spencer Stuart, the average tenure of a CMO was about 23 months in 2006. Apparently that rose to 42 months in 2011—maybe because CMOs are getting more strategic in the way they approach their jobs?—but it is still very low in some industries. Siegel+Gale just completed a survey among CMOs of Fortune 2000 companies, and when we tried to follow up with 15 of them six weeks later, four of the 15 were no longer with their companies. Perhaps this turnover is because some CMOs still use a "try it and hope" approach to branding decisions, instead of fact-based tools that increase their odds of getting it right the first time.

I also suspect that many CMOs and brand managers resist fact-based branding because they see research as complex and intimidating. While some research relies on advanced math and analytical tools, **a fundamental understanding of fact-based branding will dramatically simplify your job and the way you communicate with the market.** Fact-based branding helps you identify the things that decision makers look for when they choose products or services and what they believe to be true or untrue about your brand. These two pieces of information greatly clarify the task of crafting compelling and believable marketing messages.

Moreover, fact-based branding gives you a way to confirm—or disprove— internally derived beliefs that can sometimes be remarkably off-target. Several years ago I was asked to apply the tools described later in this book for a global heavy equipment manufacturer. The company had already identified what they believed to be the key drivers of brand preference. A rigorous analysis revealed that these assumptions were only 50 percent correct—the same percentage one would have obtained by randomly assigning key driver status. As is the case with many US firms that operate internationally, this company incorrectly assumed that what drives choice in this country drives choice in other parts of the world.

Brand consulting firms have had to adapt to this shift toward fact-based branding as well. In the mid-1990s, some of these firms started to offer research capabilities to augment the "guru" nature of their business. They took this step partly as a response to growing demand and partly as a way to differentiate themselves from their competitors. By the turn of the century, it had become an imperative.

I was hired by Siegel+Gale in 2006 with the clear mandate to build a world-class research capability. The firm realized that brand consultancies without such a capability were at a serious disadvantage when bidding on most major branding assignments. When I joined the company, it was essentially just a middleman for research, farming the design and analysis out to independent research firms who were not in touch with the brand strategy of the client. Today, Siegel+Gale has 10 statistical researchers on staff, and all design and analysis is done by these experts. Only the data collection is outsourced.

On both sides—client and consultant—fact-based branding is here to stay. CMOs today are far savvier about branding as a science than their counterparts of previous decades. Yet while most CMOs know that these tools are out there, many still don't fully understand them. Maybe they've taken steps to apply fact-based branding only to be provided with poorly executed research that wasn't even helpful.

Those CMOs and brand managers who actively develop their skills in this area and demand the same from the research professionals they work with will give themselves a clear advantage in the market. They'll make better decisions—informed by real facts—and strengthen the brands they're charged with protecting and growing. Conversely, those CMOs and brand managers who don't apply rigorous fact-driven branding principles—who continue to treat marketing as an art instead of a science—risk doing serious damage to their brands. On a more personal side (as noted above), they may also be putting their own careers in jeopardy.

10 Reasons to Embrace Fact-Based Branding

1. It builds consensus within your organization. You'll enter discussions armed with facts while others enter with opinions. In all my years of applying the modeling tools described in this book, the results almost invariably led to immediate consensus. The discussion shifted from an argument about what direction the company or brand should go in to brainstorming about the best way to implement the recommendations.

2. It could add years, if not decades, to your tenure as CMO. Fact-based branding helps you understand your audience better, develop more effective communications and brand-building initiatives, and demonstrate the value of your work with business metrics. In a nutshell, it greatly increases your odds of proposing initiatives that are likely to succeed, helping you succeed as well.

3. It differentiates between opportunities and dead ends. In the search for the ever-elusive "white space," fact-based branding can help you identify the white space that's white because it represents a unique competitive advantage rather than the space that is white because it's a losing place to be.

4. It contributes to building more persuasive brand communications. About 2,500 years ago, Aristotle wrote *Rhetoric*, probably the first great work on the art of persuasion. The book lays out three ways to get your point across, and fact-based branding supports all three. It provides reason and logic (logos) that tap into your audience's emotions about your brand (pathos), and helps you establish credibility (ethos) with that audience. These are the underpinnings of great brand communications.

5. It integrates the voice of the customer (and prospective new consumer) into your marketing and communications practices. Six Sigma organizations embrace fact-based branding for this very reason. It enables you to build a brand that is driven by what matters to buyers rather than just what matters to you. The brand can speak to what decision makers want to buy rather than what you want to sell.

6 It provides concrete metrics for evaluating the effectiveness of brand-building initiatives. IBM's 2011 Global Chief Marketing Officer Study reported that the single most important measure for gauging marketing success is estimating marketing return on investment (ROI). In the past, these metrics have been extremely difficult to develop, since the obvious yardsticks (like sales revenue) are driven by dozens of factors, not just brand initiatives. Fact-based branding lets you isolate the effect of your efforts and determine what's really working. In fact, some of the tools described in this book can allow you to predict the likely return on brand investments (ROBI) even before you implement them.

7 It greatly enhances efficiency. Branding would be so much easier if you could simply ask customers and prospects what they want. Unfortunately, you can't. Instead, you need tools that can derive this information based on how their perceptions match their purchasing actions. By allowing you to get this information in a more linear way, fact-based branding lets you focus your efforts on things that really matter to your audiences rather than wasting energy on things that don't.

8 It elevates brand and communications to a vital role within the organization. You can discuss the strategic implications of one of the company's most valuable corporate assets—its brand—using facts and figures rather than just anecdotes or opinions. When you can demonstrate how your initiatives directly affect the bottom line of the company, others will listen in a way they haven't before.

9 It helps you talk to other members of the C-Suite using their language. These tools are designed to look at brands from a business perspective. They introduce hard metrics for measuring return on investment, share of preference and other critical metrics. This is the language of business, the language of the C-Suite, and your ability to speak this language gives you credibility with your company's senior management.

10 It's really fun. Need I say more?

Chapter 2
Distinguishing Good Research from Bad Research

When I talk about using research to support branding decisions, I sometimes hear a familiar refrain: "We're already doing that." Of course you are. If a company believes in branding enough to have a CMO and brand managers, it isn't going to hamstring them by operating completely in the dark. So why should you continue to read this book? Consider the following four points:

1. Some research is valuable and some simply isn't
2. Some researchers are better than others
3. Fact-based branding can improve your ability to create a powerful brand and make your job easier
4. You need to understand research concepts well enough to discern what research is valuable and what's not

1. Some research is valuable and some simply isn't
As with most things, not all research is equal. Some research is truly powerful: its methodology is sound and it genuinely points you to the right decisions. Other research is seriously flawed and isn't worth the money you spent on it.

> Even though you likely already use research to inform your branding decisions, some research is valuable and some isn't, just as some researchers are better than others. This book is intended to help you discern the difference and become better able to use fact-based research to your greatest advantage.

As I mentioned in the foreword, part of my motivation to write this book was yet another experience with some really poor research. I don't want CMOs and brand managers to be stuck working with poor research. Not only does it lead to flawed decisions, but it taints the reputation of the profession I love.

Here are some examples of where market research can go wrong:

Researchers can talk to the wrong people
Some research looks exclusively at the existing customers of your brand. This is too narrow. If you want to understand how decision makers choose between your brand and its competitors, you cannot talk only to your own customers. They may be able to offer some insight into why they chose your brand—though likely not very well, as discussed in point 3 below—but this leaves out all the people who chose a different brand. In fact, insight into why your brand is not selected is usually far more valuable than insight into why people are already buying it. Chapter 3 talks more in depth on this topic, and it provides a framework for thinking about branding and brand research.

At the same time, some research projects take the opposite approach and target a sample that's too broad by including people who don't even buy the product or service in question. This is equally flawed. One may want to know how the brand is perceived by the general public, but I don't understand how the perceptions of non-buyers—even if it's accurate—can help CMOs better understand the buying process. And that's what branding is really all about.

Finally, truly understanding the buying process requires that we understand the environment in which those decisions get made. For example, in the business-to-business world, the end users of a product often apply different decision criteria than purchasing agents, and these two groups should not be commingled in the research. Chapter 11 discusses buying environments.

Questions can include compound attributes or have other problems

Most brand research—either acquisition research or retention research, such as customer satisfaction tracking—asks respondents to rate a brand on a series of attributes. Sometimes critical dimensions don't make it onto this list of attributes. But poorly constructed attributes also can render the results meaningless. For example, if the list includes compound attributes (i.e., those that contain more than one thought, idea or concept), how can you interpret a low rating? What part or parts of the attribute was the respondent actually rating?

Chapter 4 offers suggestions for how to construct proper attributes for brand research. It also suggests pitfalls to avoid.

The research can misidentify key brand attributes

Many research studies determine the importance of brand attributes by simply asking respondents to rate or rank them. The problem with this approach is that most decision makers simply don't know how they make choices. Decision making occurs at the subconscious level, not the conscious level, so people cannot accurately explain which attributes led to a purchase. Instead, when asked, people tend to offer answers based on:
+ what they think the interviewer wants to hear
+ what will make the decision maker sound smart or discerning
+ what's socially appropriate to say
+ how they believe they make choices

For these reasons, the **stated** importance of brand attributes is simply not sufficiently valid. Instead, we need to **derive** the actual importance of these attributes, by using appropriate statistical methods.

Other research reports base recommendations for action on the gap between perceptions of your brand and those of a competitor. As this section is suggesting, not all attributes are equally important. If a competitor is spending money to "own" an attribute that decision makers don't care about, you should celebrate this misallocation of resources rather than make the same mistake.

Chapter 10 provides an in-depth discussion of how to accurately determine the importance of attributes in decision making.

The final results may not be presented clearly

Even if research is well-designed, the presentation of results can lead to problems. For instance, the research may utilize scales with enough response options, but researchers may combine those results in ways that cloud the real implications and make it all but impossible to discern how best to respond.

Chapter 5 discusses the use of scales in brand research and offers suggestions for how results should be reported. Chapter 6 points out potential hazards that can occur if you combine or compare results across groups that use scales differently. This is particularly important for companies that conduct global research.

I could go on and on with other examples of poor research; unfortunately, there's enough of it out there.

2. Some researchers are better than others

Much of the poor research out there is the product of individuals who lack the proper training in survey research and statistical analysis. The majority of research professionals outside of academia do not have degrees in statistics, and many have little academic training apart from an undergraduate statistics course or two. As a result, many are applying statistical tools with a somewhat limited understanding of the underlying assumptions required—and what to do when those assumptions are not met. It's akin to a self-taught weekend mechanic trying to work on an Indy car.

Even with a rigorous statistical background, the real learning takes place once one starts working in the real world. Academic training provides an excellent array of tools for examining and analyzing relationships between variables and for building statistical models. However, just about all these statistical procedures are built on assumptions that rarely are met in the real world (at least in the world of brand research).

I hold a PhD in mathematical statistics. Some of my training was invaluable upon entering the workplace. I took a course in sampling theory that was probably the most useful in terms of its day-to-day application in my job. Yet not one course out of the entire program focused on how to deal with the real-life circumstances when the assumptions that underlie the statistical tools are not met. I had to learn everything I know in this regard on the job. For example, I was faced with missing data—either from respondents who didn't answer a particular question or because certain questions were not asked of everyone to reduce respondent burden—in my very first assignment as a statistician in the US Coast Guard, and I still encounter missing data almost every day. Yet none of my undergraduate or graduate courses discussed appropriate ways to deal with this real-world issue.

That fact—and seeing younger researchers without formal training face even bigger challenges in doing their jobs well—is what motivated me to write the companion volume to this book (*Fact-Based Branding in the Real World: A Simple Survival Guide for Research Professionals*). I'm sharing the lessons I've learned in the hope that others won't have to learn them by producing poor research first.

3. Fact-based branding can improve your ability to create a powerful brand and make your job easier

The techniques of fact-based branding can help you in myriad ways. Here are just a few:

Optimizing brand positioning in the market

Fact-based branding helps you identify the "compelling truth" of your brand. It identifies the attributes that matter in acquiring and/or retaining decision makers, and it marries the perceptions of those key drivers with the reality of what your brand can deliver. Chapter 10 contains a detailed discussion of identifying the attributes that matter, and Chapters 11 and 12 discuss techniques that can help you determine the business impact of alternate positioning of your brand. Chapter 19 takes this concept even further, with a means of estimating the likely ROBI of initiatives before you implement them.

These techniques can also help you resist the dangerous allure of two concepts that have gained a certain amount of cachet in marketing: "The Big Idea" and "Finding the White Space." While it's critical to break through the clutter of advertising and messaging, the mythical promises of these ideas can distract you from sound brand management. Focusing on the right messages and being consistent are as important—or more so—than finding the elusive big idea. In addition, much of the "white space" is white for the simple reason that it's not a good place to be. Chapter 15 discusses the big idea and white space.

Applying fact-based branding principles from the bottom up in an organization can both identify the optimal brand positioning for each line of business (or for each product in the case of a portfolio brand) and identify how the parent brand (i.e., the corporate brand or the portfolio brand) can provide the greatest benefit to the brands underneath it. It identifies the best way to let the parent or portfolio brand do the "heavy lifting."

Optimizing brand architecture

Decision trees can clarify how existing brands and new brands (e.g., those gained through acquisitions) should fit within your brand architecture. Fact-based branding principles can help you identify the "equity" of each brand and determine those brands that have the potential to become portfolio brands, those that should be slotted as product brands and those that are rationalization candidates.

Extending a brand and minimizing cannibalization

Fact-based branding principles can be used to assess the merits of extending a brand into a related category and to estimate the potential cannibalization that might occur as a result. For example, a Japanese pharmaceutical company used the techniques described in Chapter 12 to determine its likely success in extending its brand. The company sold the leading painkiller in pill form, and it was considering expanding into the transdermal, or "patch" market, which a competitor dominated. The research identified the key drivers of brand choice in the transdermal market as well as the current brand equity of each brand in the pill market. A simulation model revealed that the likely success of the company in the transdermal marketplace would come at a severe cost to the company's more profitable pill business.

Segmenting the market

Most segmentation studies classify the market into groups of individuals that have similar demographic and/or psychographic characteristics. This helps companies develop relevant messaging and advertising strategies to reach them. But this is a relatively simplistic approach. Fact-based branding looks beyond variables such as age or lifestyle and instead lets you segment decision makers based on how they make brand choices—the real point of brand research. Chapter 23 presents a detailed case study on preference-based segmentation.

Understanding the value of your brand

Companies spend a lot of money on brand valuation (i.e., estimating the monetary value of their brands). Yet I question whether the monetary value of a brand ever plays a role in decision makers' buying processes. Can you imagine a consumer choosing between Coke and Pepsi based on how much the brand valuation of the two brands is? Fact-based branding is about how people buy, not how CEOs brag (e.g., "My brand is worth more than your brand"). The principles outlined in this book allow you to understand how your brand helps or hurts you at the point-of-sale. Chapter 22 discusses the merits of brand valuation versus what I call brand effect.

Managing the customer experience

Brand valuation and brand effect apply to the acquisition side of the customer life cycle. The role of the brand shifts from making promises to keeping them once a prospect becomes a customer. Fact-based branding is critical to managing the customer experience. Chapter 21 discusses the relationship between customer satisfaction and customer retention.

Making your job easier

Perhaps as important as any of these advantages, fact-based branding can make your job easier. Managing a brand without any facts or concrete information—or, worse, inaccurate information—is a risky endeavor. The information that fact-based research provides can inform the brand decisions you make, improve your performance and reduce the stress that comes from managing a brand by sheer gut instinct.

4. You need to understand research concepts well enough to discern what research is valuable and what's not

It's not my intent to turn you into a statistician. As much as I'd like to think that all CMOs and brand managers have an inner statistician just yearning to break out, I realize that this isn't close to true. But I do hope this book will give you enough information to use fact-based branding to its greatest advantage and to recognize the red flags that could be signaling poor research. Finally, I hope that this book will provide you with a sufficient background that will facilitate meaningful discussions with your research professionals regarding tools that can or should be used. To that end, each chapter closes with a set of questions that you may wish to discuss with the professionals providing your research support.

Chapter 3
Brand Research and the Decision-Making Process

When you get down to it, branding is about understanding how decision makers make choices so that all your marketing materials, advertising campaigns and any other messaging can effectively communicate the attributes that will influence those purchasing decisions. As I mentioned in Chapter 2, however, you can't ascertain how people make these choices by simply asking them. For example, when asked to list the criteria they use for making a purchase decision, people almost invariably include "price" or "cost" as one of the first two answers. After all, this makes them sound discerning, and it's certainly a criterion that we're all "supposed" to apply. Yet when you look at market leaders across various industries, how often does the low-cost brand have the largest share? Why is this so rarely the case if so many people claim to use price as one of their top decision criteria? In fact, these decisions are not really about the cost alone but about perceived value for the cost. Porsche drivers and Hyundai drivers pay significantly different amounts for their cars, but both groups believe their purchase represents the appropriate value for what they paid. Yet many consumers don't express their brand preferences this way. We're taught to be price-conscious rather than value-conscious.

This phenomenon comes up again and again in research: the importance that a person assigns to an attribute (its "stated importance") doesn't accurately reflect the degree to which this attribute drives the purchasing decision. In reality, a good brand researcher can explain a person's actual buying behavior much more accurately than the buyer can.

> When you get right down to it, branding is really about understanding how individuals make decisions. Yet most decision makers truly do not know how they make choices among brands and cannot accurately explain their choices to a researcher. Their actual behavior rarely reflects the criteria they claim to use.

As an exercise, present a group of people with a list of attributes that could influence their brand preference for a particular product. Next, ask them to construct the "scorecard" they would use in rating various brands. That is, ask them to assign a weight to each attribute that reflects the importance of that attribute in their buying decision. Finally, ask each person to rate the leading brands in that category on each of the attributes, using a 10-point scale.

With those two sets of numbers—the importance weights and each brand's attribute scores—you can calculate the relative "worth" of each brand for each person. You simply multiply the weight and the brand's score for each attribute and then sum the products. In theory, the brand with the highest value should be that person's preferred brand—the one they actually choose in the real world. Yet whenever I do this exercise with real people, there's usually only a modest relationship between the two, maybe 50 percent. People's purchasing behavior doesn't agree with what they say really matters. It's as if they claim to be looking for fish but actually order a cheeseburger.

In many cases, the difficulty in understanding the decision process is further exacerbated by the challenge of identifying the decision maker. Not only do you need to ask the right questions, but you need to ask them of the right person. While this is a fairly straightforward exercise in consumer brand research, it's far more complex in the business-to-business world. Here decisions often are made by a committee. Some people analyze and recommend brands, others (either an individual or a committee) make the final selection and still others may approve the actual purchase, e.g., the division head or the chief financial officer (CFO).

The criteria that drive brand choice can vary radically depending on which person in this chain you talk to. For example, the bench scientist who will be using a mass spectrometer is likely to use very different criteria than the purchasing agent in the same company. Why? Because they are rewarded (or chastised) for different things in their jobs. The scientist needs a piece of equipment that's easy to use and performs the specific functions he or she requires better than any other piece of equipment. The purchasing agent is trying to keep costs down, often by arranging group purchase discounts. These two approaches often lead to different preferences.

I'll talk more about these different buying environments in subsequent chapters, but for now, let's reduce the complexity a bit. Assume that we're in a homogeneous buying environment—that is, one where individuals apply similar criteria to their purchasing decisions. In this situation, the role of the brand manager is to build preference among prospects and build loyalty among current customers or clients. Before getting into the more granular issues of brand research, we need a framework to understand how people make brand decisions. While the specific value structures may differ significantly among different purchasers and products (e.g., the scientist purchasing a mass spectrometer versus a teenager purchasing a smart phone), the process that decision makers go through is remarkably consistent. As Exhibit 3.1 depicts, almost any decision maker goes through a five-gate process.

Gate 1 is basic awareness of the brand. It addresses the question, "Has the buyer heard of the brand?" As a decision maker, if I'm not aware of a brand, it plays no role in my selection. That is, I'm neither seeking it nor giving it an advantage. Research consistently shows that consumers are more likely to purchase a product from a company they've heard of compared to the same

Exhibit 3.1 The decision making process

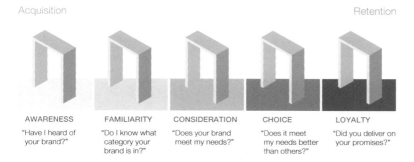

Acquisition   Retention

AWARENESS   FAMILIARITY   CONSIDERATION   CHOICE   LOYALTY

"Have I heard of   "Do I know what   "Does your brand   "Does it meet   "Did you deliver on
your brand?"   category your   meet my needs?"   my needs better   your promises?"
                     brand is in?"   than others?"

product from a company they haven't heard of, even if they know almost nothing about the company other than its name.

That said, lack of awareness doesn't mean I won't buy the product or service. The brand may be an "invisible" or "ingredient" brand that doesn't directly target customers. This is frequently the case with business-to-business brands. Sometimes the companies that own such brands debate whether it's worth increasing their awareness among end customers. For example, BASF spent considerable money on a mass advertising campaign to tell consumers, "At BASF, we don't make a lot of the things you buy; we make a lot of the things you buy better." Of course, one of the best known brands to go from invisible to demanded as an ingredient brand is Intel.

Another case where the brand plays little or no role in the purchase process is a classic commodity product, like nails at the local hardware store. I'm a do-it-yourselfer at home, yet I couldn't tell you who manufactures the nails I have in my workshop if my life depended on it. I simply buy the brand that Home Depot or my local hardware store has on the shelves. Or I may buy an unknown brand because it looks solid or has attractive packaging, or some other factor at the point of purchase. But it wasn't because of the brand.

Gate 2 in the framework is familiarity. It addresses the question, "Does the buyer know what the brand does?" As with Gate 1, if the buyer does not know what category the brand is in (e.g., food processing equipment), he or she will not actively buy it because of its brand. When Bell Laboratories was transformed into Lucent back in the mid-1990s, the new company—a classic business-to-business brand—spent a rumored $100 million to build its brand awareness through mass media advertising. It developed a red circle logo that famously resembled a coffee mug stain. Household awareness of the name and its logo soared, but how many households knew what Lucent actually did? That is, how many households were truly familiar with the brand? (And, one could argue, why should consumers even care, since Lucent is a business-to-business brand and ordinary consumers presumably weren't its target audience anyway?)

If a brand succeeds in making it through Gates 1 and 2, it has, at least theoretically, made it onto the buyer's long list for consideration. The decision maker has heard of the brand and knows that it operates in the product or service category that he or she is seeking. Gate 3 is consideration. It addresses the question, "Does the brand meet the buyer's specific needs?"

In many years of modeling purchase decisions, I've found that Gate 3 is a predominantly rational process and one in which brand perceptions are critical. At Gate 3, buyers evaluate brands at a relatively "macro" level by doing the requisite due diligence. For example, if you're buying a car, you may eliminate brands at Gate 3 because they cost more than $40,000 or less than $25,000. You may do Internet searches, look at brochures, read reviews and talk to friends about their car purchases—lots of rational fact-finding.

If a brand makes it through Gate 3, it is now on the short list—one of up to three or so brands that the buyer is seriously considering for the final selection. But while Gate 3 tends to be a rational, information-driven evaluation, the next step in the purchasing process is far more emotional.

Gate 4 is choice. It addresses the question, "Does the brand meet the buyer's needs *better than any other brand*?" This is often a subjective decision. The rational due diligence of Gate 3 gets the buyer to a point where he or she realizes that any of the brands on the short list will do the job. At Gate 4, the buyer is free to choose the brand he or she simply likes the best.

The primary use of rational criteria at Gate 3 and emotional criteria at Gate 4 applies even in pure, business-to-business decisions involving significant sums. Many years ago, a major manufacturer of corporate jets was having problems closing deals. The company designed some of the finest jets on the market, and it always made it through Gate 3 to the final round of consideration. Yet it almost always lost the final sale (Gate 4). The company couldn't understand why this was happening so frequently, and it hired a brand consulting firm to understand what was going wrong.

The answer turned out to be fairly simple. The company was run by engineers, and they thought like engineers. They felt that because they excelled on the design aspects of the product, they should lead the market—or at least command a much greater share than they were currently winning. Yet in focusing so intensely on the rational side of the decision, they failed to realize the importance of the emotional side. In fact, the final purchasing decision was often made by a CEO who was very aware of the emotional projection of different brands of corporate jets. In essence, the final decision was often made based on which brand the CEO—in conversations with other CEOs on the golf course—could say he or she flew in on. It was about status.

Another common example comes in the evaluation process for management consulting firms. When these firms pitch themselves to corporate clients, they usually provide a proposal (Gate 3). If the firm makes it through that gate successfully, it's invited to make an in-person presentation (Gate 4). All too often, these firms make the mistake of simply restating their proposal during the presentation. Why do these firms do that? Do they think the potential clients didn't read the proposal? Those people don't need to hear the firm's capabilities again. If they weren't convinced that the firm could do the job, they wouldn't have invited the firm back for a final presentation. Instead, what the potential client wants is to meet the people who will be working on the job, and to determine if the "fit" is right. Those people in the conference room want some reassurance that things won't go wrong. In short, they want to see which team they like the most.

Once through Gate 4, the prospect becomes a customer or client. **Gate 5** represents the ongoing customer or client relationship. It addresses the question, "Does the brand live up to its promise?" Gate 5 is essentially a series of decisions that customers make. Should they purchase additional products? Increase share of wallet within the existing product category? Continue the relationship with the brand at all? If a brand can successfully pull a customer or client through Gate 5, it's rewarded with loyalty.

Brand research: A composite of acquisition and retention research
The decision process depicted Exhibit 3.1 covers the entire life cycle of a customer's relationship with a brand, from initial prospect to customer to loyal customer. The first four gates describe the customer **acquisition** stage, while the final gate represents the customer **retention** stage. These are the two major branches of brand research: customer acquisition research and customer retention research (which also includes expanding the customer relationship).

> **Branding covers the entire customer life cycle, from acquisition through retention. From a brand research standpoint, customer acquisition and customer retention are linked by the fact that in most categories, branding is a zero-sum game: unless the buyer is new to the category, one brand's acquisition at Gate 4 is another brand's attrition at Gate 5.**

There's a more profound link between the acquisition and retention stages and the research that supports them: unless the buyer is new to the category or the brand operates in a multiple brand usage environment, **one brand's acquisition at Gate 4 is another brand's attrition loss at Gate 5.** The only question is whether the new brand won that consumer (which falls under brand or customer acquisition research) or the former brand lost that consumer (which falls under customer relationship management and customer satisfaction research).

Chief marketing officers, brand managers and brand researchers need to consider both sides of this relationship. If you focus solely on acquisition, you fail to recognize the importance of retaining customers and expanding that relationship by increasing your share of wallet and/or selling them additional products. You also limit your ability to understand whether you're living up to your implicit promises during the sales process. At the same time, if you focus solely on retention—particularly just customer satisfaction—you leave yourself vulnerable to competitors who are trying to steal your customers.

There are clear distinctions between the customer acquisition process and the retention/relationship expansion process, and these differences have profound implications for the research that supports them. First, by its very nature, acquisition research considers the entire marketplace for a product or service—both new prospects and current customers. In contrast, retention research focuses primarily on a brand's existing customer base. If you want to understand which brand is delivering the best customer experience, you should measure satisfaction among your competitors' customers as well. But even here you should focus on customers of a specified brand, not its prospects.

This leads to a second distinction between the two types of research: the level of attributes that you should consider. Because acquisition research covers both customers and prospects, it must focus on attributes that non-customers can rate. That is, acquisition attributes must be less-detailed than customer satisfaction or retention attributes. If a bank branch wanted to study customer satisfaction, it could use an attribute like "Employees address me by name when I visit." But prospects likely wouldn't have an opinion on this attribute as they may not have set foot inside the branch. (In some cases, a bank may make personal greetings a centerpiece of its brand positioning and heavily advertise the fact until even non-customers know it, but those situations are rare.) Instead, a higher-level attribute that might work for both prospects and customers alike is to ask whether the branch "is customer-oriented." It's a less-detailed attribute, and even non-customers will likely have some perception on whether this is true.

Summary
Branding is fundamentally about understanding how customers make decisions and then communicating and delivering on the messages that are most relevant to those customers. Simply asking people how they make choices often results in very misleading information. Instead, you have to apply sound methods for determining where customers are in the buying process, and how they make the choice to advance to the next stage.

It's important to understand how customer acquisition and customer retention fit together and to ensure that a fact-based brand management program properly integrates both components. If you focus only on customer satisfaction, you're not using fact-based tools to inform your acquisition activities and are likely to miss critical opportunities. If you don't include customer satisfaction as part of your brand management, you limit your ability to assess whether the customer experience is living up to what your brand promised in the sales process.

This five-step framework of how decisions are made along the customer life cycle can be extremely valuable, not only in brand management but in developing general sales and marketing strategies. If you map the key drivers of brand preference onto the various gates, where customers use them to make decisions, you'll have a better understanding of the elements the brand must promote at each step in the sales and marketing process.

Questions to discuss with your research professionals

+ How does the framework presented in this chapter apply to our brand?
+ How are we determining which brand attributes matter to the decision makers who buy our products and services?
+ If we're using stated importance, why are we doing that? Can't we find more accurate ways of determining how customers choose our brand?
+ Do we understand how people make decisions at each gate in the framework?
+ Are we adequately researching the acquisition component of the customer life cycle?
+ Are we including both customers and non-customers in our acquisition research?
+ Are the attributes included in our acquisition research appropriate for both customers and prospects? Can potential buyers—who know about our brand but don't have direct experience with it— rate it on the attributes we're using as they're currently worded?
+ Are we studying our competitors' customers as well as our own? Do we know what we have to overcome to win those customers over?

Chapter 4
Developing Brand Attributes

Brand attributes are curiously powerful things. They're the building blocks of fact-based branding. Constructed correctly, they can tap into perceptions about the brand that customers and prospects didn't even know they felt. However, if they're not carefully constructed—as is the case in a lot of bad market research—brand attributes will only confuse people.

Marketers have to weigh two considerations in assessing whether a brand attribute is appropriate: the level of detail and the objective. Regarding the first consideration, level of detail, the information in the attribute needs to be as detailed as possible while still allowing the respondent to rate the brand on it. Greater detail helps you understand how to act on the results. On the other hand, if an attribute is too detailed and goes beyond the level at which the respondent interacts with the brand, you're likely to get no response, or—worse—nonsensical answers. (Recall the bank branch example in the last chapter—"Employees greet me by name when I visit" is a detailed attribute that only current customers would be likely to answer. Conversely, a broader attribute with less detail allows all respondents to answer, such as whether the bank "is customer-oriented.")

In addition to the level of detail, marketers also have to consider the objective, or purpose, of the attribute. Acquisition research typically focuses on the positioning of a brand, or on its perceived "equities." (The term "brand equities" has a somewhat fuzzy definition in brand research. To clarify, I use it to refer to the **competitive advantages of a brand that decision makers find compelling**.) Conversely, retention or customer satisfaction research typically focuses on the actual customer experience. As a result, acquisition attributes should focus on potential factors that drive brand preference—why a customer chooses Brand A over Brand B—while retention attributes should focus on the customer experience at each important touch point between the customer and the brand.

> Marketers need to consider two factors in constructing brand attributes: their level of detail and their objective. The information embodied in the attribute should be as detailed as possible while still enabling a respondent to rate the brand on it.

Let's focus on acquisition attributes first. As mentioned earlier, we need to keep these attributes at a level at which non-customers can relate with respect to the brand. Within that constraint, how can we construct a list of potential attributes that drive a customer's preference for a brand in a specific category?

One way is to hold focus groups or in-depth interviews with both customers and prospects. This can provide insight on how actual decision makers assess brands in your category. Focus groups are particularly valuable if you are a reasonably new entrant into the category. Yet people in

Acquisition attributes should focus on potential factors that drive brand preference, while retention or customer satisfaction attributes should focus on the customer experience at each important touch point between the customer and the brand.

these research formats tend to focus on the obvious attributes (e.g., price, convenience, quality, reliability, service). You can also talk to people within your company—such as product managers, R&D departments, sales managers, among others—but they're likely to focus too heavily on specific features of the product or service. They're like the engineers at the private-jet manufacturer I mentioned earlier, who thought that the plane with the best technical specifications would always win in the market.

In fact, manufacturing companies tend to confuse brand research with product research. When these companies assemble a list of brand attributes, nine of out ten are specific features and benefits of the product. This makes it very difficult for the company to understand the role of "brand" in the purchase decision or to understand the role of other key factors, such as processes or intangibles.

Product features and benefits are important, as they represent the rational side of the purchase decision, but brand attributes also need to represent the emotional side.

Difficulties in constructing brand attributes come up in business-to-business environments as well. Some people accept the premise that consumer product purchase decisions include emotional elements, but they think business-to-business purchases are purely rational decisions. **The fact is, both types of attributes—rational and emotional—drive virtually every purchasing decision.**

Eight major categories of acquisition attributes

While brand attributes may seem like a large and unwieldy topic, a structured approach will help you put them into perspective. Let's start with acquisition attributes. Exhibit 4.1 shows the eight major categories of acquisition attributes. The lines between these eight can get somewhat blurry, yet this list provides a structured approach to developing attributes for the entire market. It also helps you build positioning maps to determine how different brands are seen in the marketplace. I'll talk more about each of these eight.

In constructing brand attributes, ensure that you apply the tenets of simplicity (e.g., clear, succinct, meaningful, human) and express them in the voice of the prospective customer.

24

Exhibit 4.1 Eight major categories of acquisition attributes

1 infrastructure
2 products/services
3 process/approach
4 people/skills
5 mission/purpose
6 emotional connection
7 emotional projection
8 personality

**1. Infrastructure attributes address the question,
"What does the brand have?"**
It includes "countable" factors, like the number of branches a bank owns, the number of routes an airline flies, the total assets under management for a financial services firm and so on. Companies like Visa successfully use infrastructure as the lead thought in their positioning ("We're everywhere you want to be"). Examples of infrastructure attributes include:
+ Operates a broad global network that covers all the locations I need
+ Offers convenient hours of operation, including weekends
+ Is financially strong and secure
+ Is available at convenience stores throughout the country

**2. Products/Services attributes address the question,
"What does the brand do?"**
This category is where the product development people have their say, as it's really assessing how well the company's offerings function. For example, General Electric has built a strong brand around the attributes of dependability, quality and reliability and will not put its brand on any product that does not deliver these attributes. Hence, the GE brand is more about its products than its infrastructure or its selling approach. Examples of products/services attributes include:
+ Offers a complete range of financial products and services
+ Manufactures equipment with superior fuel efficiency
+ Offers a wide range of flavors
+ Manufactures durable equipment
+ Produces superior products

3. Process/Approach attributes examine the question, "How does the brand do what it does?"

Netflix completely unseated Blockbuster by distributing the same product in a much more convenient manner—eliminating the dual annoyances of travel to the video store and late fees. Certain management consulting firms are known for their processes, while others are known more for the skill of their individual consultants. Examples of process/approach attributes include:

+ Builds strong relationships with customers
+ Provides good value for the cost
+ Offers superior customer service
+ Is easy to do business with
+ Develops innovative solutions that respond to client needs

4. People/Skills attributes address the question, "Who does the brand have?"

In some environments, people are very visible, and this can be a powerful differentiator. Two brands that have traditionally been perceived as having superior people and skills are Goldman Sachs and McKinsey. Even though people come to those firms from competitors and leave those firms to go to competitors—as is the case in almost any category—those two firms manage their brands to maintain an aura of superiority in this area. Examples of people/skills attributes include:

+ Has highly knowledgeable sales representatives
+ Has specialized expertise in offshore exploration
+ Has strong management
+ Attracts the best and brightest talent
+ Has consultants with superior presentation skills

5. Mission/Purpose attributes address the question, "Why does the brand do what it does?"

This is a complex area in which attributes may be relatively scarce. However, some brands have successfully built their market position around this area. For example, Disney does not position itself around its theme parks or movies (infrastructure or products/services); instead it's positioned around great family entertainment (purpose). Companies like The Body Shop use environmentalism to position themselves around their mission.

The problem with many potential mission/purpose attributes is that they may be no more than reflections of the category. "Cares about your health" doesn't work as a differentiating attribute in the health care field, because that's part of the very definition of the category itself. Still, some companies are able to construct mission/purpose attributes, such as:

+ Is an advocate for patients' rights
+ Is an agent of change
+ Gives back to the communities in which it operates
+ Shows concern for the environment

6. Emotional connection attributes address the question, "How does the brand make me feel?"

These attributes can reflect physical or emotional ways in which the product or brand resonates with the decision maker, or they can represent the sense that the product or brand shares the decision maker's values. Examples of emotional connection attributes include:
+ Gives me peace of mind
+ Is designed for people like me
+ Helps me to be creative in my job
+ Makes me feel successful

7. Emotional projection attributes are relevant to the question, "What does my use of the brand say about me to others?"

These attributes are particularly relevant to luxury brands like Rolex, BMW and Cartier, but they also can apply to businesses (e.g., "Successful companies run SAP"). Examples of emotional projection attributes include:
+ Makes me look fashionable
+ Is a brand used by successful companies
+ Is the brand that knowledgeable people choose

8. Personality attributes address the question, "How does the brand present itself?"

As I mentioned earlier, almost every decision has a significant emotional component, and a company's personality plays an important role in this regard. Consider Apple's long-running television campaign that played on the perceived personality differences between itself (laid-back, informal) and PC manufacturers (staid, corporate). Examples of brand personality traits include:
+ Is responsive
+ Is flexible
+ Is visionary
+ Is conservative
+ Is innovative

Customer satisfaction/retention attributes

Compared to customer acquisition research, the attributes used in customer satisfaction or retention research can be far more detailed and granular—after all, your customers already have direct experience with

Exhibit 4.2 Four channels of brand communication

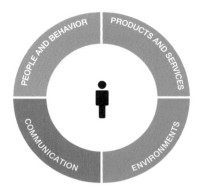

your product or service, giving you a far greater range of issues to evaluate. Accordingly, these attributes should focus on the customer at the most important "touch points," or interactions with the brand.

These touch points generally fall into four principal channels, as shown in Exhibit 4.2. Other factors can shape people's perceptions of a brand—such as word-of-mouth, analyst reports and press coverage—yet those lie outside the control of the company or brand. These four channels, by contrast, are directly within its control.

The **environments** channel includes both physical and virtual environments. A bank expresses its brand every time someone walks into one of its branch offices or visits one of its ATMs. The same holds true anytime someone visits its website or calls its 800 number to request an account balance.

The **people and behavior** channel includes front-line employees such as cashiers, customer service representatives and sales representatives. However, it also includes the CEO when he or she makes a speech, the board of directors anytime it approves an action and the entire employee base whenever there's a scandal or someone does something heroic or otherwise newsworthy.

Products and services reflect the brand by the way they look, perform and last. And virtually every form of written **communication**—business cards, welcome letters, advertisements, brochures, billing statements, etc.—is a reflection of the brand and serves as an opportunity to either reinforce the brand's inherent promise or undermine it.

All these examples are touch points—interactions between a brand and its customers—and they're areas that customer satisfaction attributes need to address. Customer satisfaction questionnaires typically are built around touch points, and they operate on several levels. At the highest level, attributes should look at the customer's overall level of satisfaction with the brand. At the second level, they should include the incidence or frequency of contact with the touch point as well as satisfaction with that particular experience. For each touch point, the third layer could look at specific aspects of service during that experience. The questionnaire also should include outcome metrics, such as the likelihood that the customer would recommend the brand to others, remain a customer, purchase additional products and so on. (This last group of metrics is important for modeling overall satisfaction.)

For example, attributes relating to the customer service function might include ratings of:
+ The customer's ability to reach a representative quickly and easily
+ The service representative's knowledge
+ The service representative's ability to explain things clearly
+ The service representative's level of courtesy
+ The extent to which the service representative
  listened to and understood the issue
+ The service representative's ability to resolve the
  problem or inquiry on the first call
+ The service representative's responsiveness in following up and providing
  an answer in those cases where he/she could not resolve it on the first call
+ The company's timeliness in resolving the issue

You may wish to include broader attributes that evaluate how well the touch point supports your brand's promise and reflects its overall personality, such as:
+ The service experience reflects a brand that puts people ahead of profits
+ The company uses technology in innovative ways to assist its
  service representatives in helping customers with inquiries

And finally, you may wish to include attributes that reflect how well the touch point adds value for consumers:
+ The service experience demonstrated the value of being a customer
+ The customer service representative made my account
  more understandable than it was before the contact

Notice how different these attributes are from the customer acquisition attributes described earlier in the chapter. Non-customers simply wouldn't be able to answer most of these questions. The two categories of research are related but substantially different in the execution.

Avoid the use of binary attributes
If you ask customers or prospects to rate a brand on a series of attributes using a 5- or 7- or 10-point scale, you have to construct the attribute accordingly so that it can be answered in varying degrees. For example, consider the brand

attribute, "Does business outside the US." This can have only two answers: yes or no. The brand either does business outside the US or it doesn't; there's no other option. This is what's called a "binary" attribute—it's a yes-or-no determination. Rating scales with more than two options are not appropriate for binary attributes.

Usually, this comes down to the language you use in constructing the attribute. An alternative to "Does business outside the US" might be "Does business in the countries that are most important to our business." A decision maker could say, "Well, sort of" and give the attribute a moderate rating. Even an attribute such as "Is global" could be interpreted as non-binary, because a brand operating in 12 countries is theoretically more global than one operating in only two countries.

Similarly the attribute "Is innovative" is not binary. The brand can be perceived as being very innovative, somewhat innovative or not very innovative at all. This level of detail in constructing brand attributes you track is very important to ensuring that you get valuable information from the research. You need to be able to act on the results and use the data in sophisticated statistical modeling or analysis. Binary attributes don't allow this.

Avoid the use of compound attributes

It's also important that each attribute addresses a single idea. Consider the attribute "The representative was knowledgeable and helpful." A high rating suggests that the representative was both knowledgeable and helpful, but what if the customer provides a moderate or low rating? Was it because the representative was knowledgeable but not helpful? The other way around? Neither? We would have no way of knowing what the respondent is really telling us.

This doesn't mean you can never use the word "and." For example, the attribute "Is financially strong and stable" isn't necessarily compound, because the two descriptors are complementary rather than discrete.

Questions to discuss with your research professionals

+ In our acquisition research, have we covered all the attributes that might drive brand preference?
+ Are we examining potential drivers of brand preference that represent reasons why our brand wins—and also why it loses?
+ Does our customer satisfaction research adequately cover the most important touch points between our brands and our customers?
+ Are we constructing attributes properly so that they're neither binary nor compound?
+ Are we phrasing our attributes with an appropriate level of detail—less detail for acquisition research and more detail for customer satisfaction/experience research?

Chapter 5
Selecting Scales to Use in Rating Brand Attributes

Any brand research or customer satisfaction program requires that people answer questions about your products or services, and the range of options you give them, i.e., the scale of possible responses, is a critical part of survey design. That choice will influence the way people respond and if they respond at all. (Too many options and they're likely to stop halfway through.) More important, your choice of a response scale impacts the way you can analyze the results and the validity of your findings.

> When developing a questionnaire to measure brand attributes in either customer acquisition or customer retention research, what scales should you use and how should you group the various responses? This is an important choice as it influences how people respond, the way you analyze the results and their validity.

Organizations use many different types of scales today, but the most common are versions of the "Likert scale" (named after an organizational psychologist named Rensis Likert, who developed the scale in the 1930s). Likert scales give survey respondents a number of options to choose from. Exhibit 5.1 shows four different scales that organizations can use to elicit responses to questions such as, "How satisfied are you with the service you receive?" (Scales A, B and D) or "How would you rate the quality of the service you receive?" (Scale C).

The first three examples are "fully anchored." That is, each point of the scale gets its own specific verbal description. "Partially anchored" scales define only some response options—typically just the end points, or the end points and the mid-point. I don't recommend using unanchored scales (which define none of the points), as they complicate the challenge of interpreting the results.

The scales in Exhibit 5.1 are designed for use in customer satisfaction research, but similar scales are used in brand tracking or acquisition research as well. For example, the anchors on the 10-point partially anchored scale could be "Completely Describes the Brand" and "Does Not Describe the Brand At All."

One of the advantages of Likert scales is that they describe a customer state in terms of a specific level of satisfaction. They also peg subjective feelings to quantifiable metrics, so that you can run statistical analyses on the answers. There are disadvantages as well, however. Larger scales (i.e., those with more options) contain so many categories that you will usually need to combine

Exhibit 5.1 Variations of Likert scales

Scale A	7-point fully anchored		Scale B	5-point fully anchored
7	very satisfied		5	very satisfied
6	satisfied		4	satisfied
5	somewhat satisfied		3	neither satisfied nor dissatisfied
4	neither satisfied nor dissatisfied		2	dissatisfied
3	somewhat dissatisfied		1	very dissatisfied
2	dissatisfied			
1	very dissatisfied			

Scale C	4-point fully anchored		Scale D	10-point partially anchored
4	excellent		10	very satisfied
3	good		9	
2	fair		8	
1	poor		7	
			6	
			5	
			4	
			3	
			2	
			1	very dissatisfied

responses into groups or present the results as a mean. (We'll talk about recommendations for optimal groupings of these scales later in this chapter.) In addition, some people are easier to satisfy than others, so these scales don't define an absolute level of service that you're providing—just how it's being received using a judgmental, relative metric.

An alternate approach is to use semantic scales. Exhibit 5.2 shows an example of a semantic scale. Global research giant Research International (now part of TNS) built semantic scales into a unique customer satisfaction measurement process called SMART (Salient Multi-Attribute Research Technique). SMART used trade-off techniques to estimate the "value" of delivery levels associated with each scale point. In that way, it could help companies identify where their effort to improve customer satisfaction would yield the greatest return on investment.

A clear advantage of the semantic scale is its ability to more accurately reflect the actual customer experience, rather than just his or her reaction to it.

Exhibit 5.2 Example of a semantic scale

"I'm going to read you four levels of performance that relate to the time it took to handle your request. After I've read all four, please tell me which one best describes your recent experience."

Level 1   The call took less time than I expected. The representative immediately understood what I needed and took care of my request rapidly.

Level 2   The call took about as long as I expected. The representative asked me several questions but took care of everything while I was on the line.

Level 3   I was on the line with the representative longer than seemed necessary. He or she seemed to be having trouble finding the information to help me.

Level 4   It took forever for him or her to figure out how to help me. It must have been the representative's first day on the job.

With semantic scales, we do not have to guess what a "7" means versus an "8."

On the other hand, semantic scales can be very difficult to construct. A customer experience at a single touch point could result in hundreds of different descriptions. Which ones do you choose for the survey? (This is one of the reasons that semantic scales are so rare in customer satisfaction research today.) Research International often tried to get around this problem by constructing one level that's aspirational (i.e., one that would "delight" the customer), another that meets the expected standard, a third that falls somewhat short of the standard without being a complete disaster and one that represents a service failure.

Reporting the results of scaled ratings

As I mentioned above, your choice of a response scale will have clear implications for how you can report the results. For a Likert or semantic scale with four or fewer possible response options, the obvious procedure is to report the percent of respondents that provided each response. But what about Likert scales that involve five or more response options?

Many researchers prefer to report the mean score in such cases. This has its advantages and disadvantages. Means are simple to calculate and present the result as a single statistic rather than grouping the results into categories that require multiple numbers to convey. On the other hand, means can actually oversimplify things a bit. Increasing a respondent's score from a 1 to a 2 has the same effect on the mean score as increasing the score from a 7 to an 8. Yet the business impact of one increase may be significantly different from the other. Hence, mean scores can mask important information.

Another consideration is that mean scores tend to be close together, even though the differences may be statistically significant. This is particularly true with 10-point customer satisfaction scales, where respondents rarely use the ratings of 1 through 4, and where many respondents refuse to award a score of 10 on principle. It's like they're the tough gymnastics judges at the Olympics. As a result, the "effective" range of means using the 10-point Likert scale is usually only about 6.0 to 8.5. (This rule of thumb doesn't hold true among low-interest categories or among some cultures; I'll discuss this more in the next chapter.) And with Likert scales of fewer than 10 points, the effective range of the means is bunched even tighter.

Mathematically, this shouldn't matter, but in practice it does. Executives who don't have statistical training often have a hard time appreciating that a change of two- or three-tenths of a percentage point, for example, can be statistically significant. It's even more difficult for these executives to believe that such a small difference can have significant business implications.

What are the alternatives to presenting results, besides citing every response category or showing the mean response (or both)? Most researchers group the responses into categories. If they have to present a single statistic with such a categorization, they typically report out the "top box" or "top two box" percentage. This refers to the percent of the respondents who provided the highest rating (top box) or one of the top two ratings (top two box).

This type of categorization has some clear advantages over the mean. First, it avoids the problem of calculating means on a scale that is not interval in nature (i.e., one in which the difference between a 1 and a 2 is identical to the difference between a 7 and an 8). By presenting groupings of responses, the scale need only be ordinal in nature. That is, the response options need only be sequential.

In addition, as long as the scale has enough points in it, grouping the results into categories tends to produce scores that have a wider range than the mean produces. For example, the top two boxes using a 7-point fully anchored Likert scale in a customer satisfaction application usually include between 50 and 85 percent of the respondents. This often has greater credibility with managers than simple means with an effective range that's only a few points wide.

So which scale should your organization use, and how should you group the responses? Like so much of market research, the answer to both questions is: it depends. The choice of scale depends on which scores fit best together and link to key outcome measures. The choice of response groupings should produce a net satisfaction score that a company can "manage on the margin." That is, it should leave room for measurable improvements. After all, the point of this research isn't simply to measure satisfaction; you're trying to measure something so that you can manage and improve it.

You should choose a scale and combine responses in reporting based on how the scores link to key outcome measures. Also, you don't want to group so many responses together that you no longer leave room for improvement.

These two factors—the type of scale and the grouping of responses—are critical aspects of survey design, yet I see many researchers making choices that don't yield useful results. For example, some companies use a 4-point fully anchored scale and combine the top two responses to calculate the percentage of "satisfied" respondents. The typical score using this algorithm is in the 90–95 percent range. There are a couple of clear problems with this approach.

First, a 4-point scale is very limited. Respondents often want to provide more precise information than this, and you lose a fair amount of information by forcing their responses into only four categories. Second, using a procedure that puts 90–95 percent of customers into the same, positive outcome means that most of the company's efforts to improve customer satisfaction are effectively addressing only 5–10 percent of its customers. Finally, scores in the 90–95 percent range don't tend to provide a lot of insight into where and how to improve.

Exhibit 5.3 Relationship between customer satisfaction level and likelihood to recommend a brand

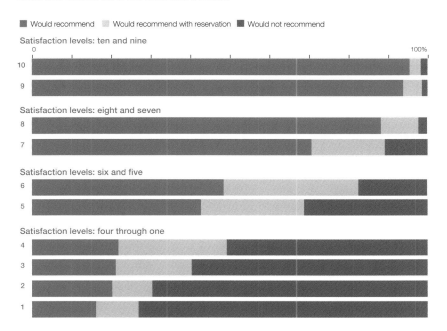

For these reasons, I recommend the use of 7- or 10-point scales (or, at a minimum, a 5-point scale). In addition, to generate actionable results, I recommend either reporting mean scores or groupings of responses.

Fortunately, it's relatively easy to determine how best to group the data. Begin by cross-tabulating the full scale responses against key outcome variables, such as "likelihood to recommend the company to others," "likelihood to continue doing business with the company for the next two years," etc. Exhibit 5.3 shows an example of such a cross-tabulation. It represents the combined results from a customer satisfaction survey for a business-to-business client, using a 10-point scale.

In this case, the groupings are pretty clear. The recommendation pattern of customers who rate their satisfaction as 9 is very similar to the pattern of those who rate their satisfaction as 10. Other natural groupings are 5–6 and 1–4. It's not as clear where the 8s belong, but other tables of this nature usually show that 7–8 is the other natural grouping. In fact, these groupings show up again and again in survey analysis in many different environments. If you wanted to present the findings in three groupings instead of four, the logical categories are 8–10, 5–7 and 1–4.

Exhibit 5.4 shows the same data in the example above—using a 10-point scale—grouped according to different categorization schemes. Note that the percentages for each category meet the criterion of being manageable on the margin. That is, no percentage is so large that it can't be used, nor is any so small that it's meaningless from a management standpoint.

Exhibit 5.4 Satisfaction levels, by combined category

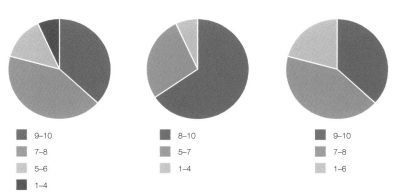

■	9–10	■	8–10	■	9–10
■	7–8	■	5–7	■	7–8
■	5–6	■	1–4	■	1–6
■	1–4				

Similarly, for a 7-point scale, if you run enough analyses you'll see that most data sets naturally fall into a fairly typical clustering:

+ **Net Satisfied** = Very Satisfied + Satisfied (6–7 on the scale)
+ **Net Neutral** = Somewhat Satisfied + Neither Satisfied
   Nor Dissatisfied (4–5 on the scale)
+ **Net Dissatisfied** = Somewhat Dissatisfied + Dissatisfied + Very
   Dissatisfied (1–3 on the scale)

Net Promoter Score

Many companies today use the Net Promoter Score (NPS) as their key customer satisfaction metric. Developed by former Bain consultant Frederick Reicheld, NPS uses an 11-point Likert scale (Reicheld includes 0) and groups the results into three categories: Promoters (9–10), Passives (7–8) and Detractors (0–6).

There's one other calculation: a brand's NPS is the percentage of Promoters minus the percentage of Detractors. This leads to a single metric that can range from −100 (all Detractors) to +100 (all Promoters). Some argue that NPS rounds off the corners a bit. For example, it combines customers who provide a lukewarm rating of 6 with an obviously irate rating of 0 or 1. The counterargument is that neither rating reflects the customer outcome that a company should desire. They can both be classified as negative, and the question of how negative doesn't really matter.

Summary

The choice of what scale to use in brand research and how to group response categories has a big impact on your ability to manage the results. Poor survey construction can make a mediocre brand look good—or a good brand look great. Not only does this artificially inflate your perception of the brand, but it severely limits your ability to develop initiatives that can improve brand perceptions or the customer experience. If you don't plan to report all response options—or report a mean response—you should group them based on how they connect to business-related outcome variables. In a nutshell, group responses together that are associated with similar behavioral outcomes.

Questions to discuss with your research professionals

+ What scales are we using in our brand research?
+ Why did we choose those scales?
+ How are we reporting the results?
+ If we are not using means to report the results, how did
   we decide which responses to group together? Have we
   conducted any analyses to ensure that the grouped responses

really summarize similar respondent behaviors?
+ Are the groupings producing percentages that are too high, thereby making it difficult to improve performance? (A customer satisfaction score of 95% satisfied customers sounds good, but it leaves only 5% of the customers as targets for initiatives.)
+ Should we change the scales we use or the way we report results? If yes, how can we transition so that it doesn't unnecessarily disrupt tracking?

Chapter 6
The Use of Scales in Global Research

Given that many companies operate globally, market research for an individual brand often crosses borders. This leads to complications, because some cultures apply scales differently than others. Simply comparing unadjusted means or top two box satisfaction levels can result in misleading conclusions. In fact, the culture providing the lower score may actually be more satisfied with the brand, or have more positive perceptions of the product or service you're trying to assess. So how can we account for these variations and determine genuine differences in satisfaction or perceptions regarding a brand?

> The mean rating from a Hispanic-culture sample is likely to be considerably higher than that derived from a non-Hispanic culture sample for the same level of service. That is, a rating of 9 (on a 10-point scale) provided by a respondent from a Hispanic-culture may not reflect the same satisfaction level coming from a Japanese respondent.

In the accompanying volume of this book, *Fact-Based Branding in the Real World: A Simple Survival Guide for Research Professionals*, I describe in detail some research that looked at this issue. Respondents from several cultures were asked to evaluate their satisfaction with service from their telephone company.

For each aspect of service, the survey used two scales. Respondents were asked to rate the service they received using a verbal or semantic scale, and to rate their overall satisfaction with the service using a 10-point Likert scale. One scale was used to calibrate the other.

The research confirmed that respondents from some Hispanic cultures tend to use the upper end of Likert scales with greater frequency while some Asian cultures—particularly the Japanese culture—are much more likely to stick to the middle range of the scale. For example, for one aspect of service rated using a 10-point scale, the mean satisfaction score provided by Hispanic respondents was 8.91. However, if these respondents had applied the scale the same way that other respondents did, the mean would actually have been 8.41, a major difference.

The research demonstrates that the use of the 9–10 range by respondents born in the US is essentially equivalent to foreign-born Hispanic respondents' use of 10 alone. Similarly, ratings of 6–8 among US-born respondents are equivalent to ratings of 8–9 among the Hispanic sample born outside the US.

Exhibit 6.1 Mean adjustment factors for various cultures

Culture	Actual mean	Adjustment factor	Adjusted mean
US-born culture	8.84	1.000	8.84
Japanese	8.52	1.028	8.77
Korean	8.43	1.059	8.93
Chinese (Mandarin)	8.17	1.033	8.44
Russian	9.38	0.963	9.04

Examples from other cultures

The study examined several additional cultures, as shown in Exhibit 6.1. The figures are based on a composite profile of seven different attributes. Combining scores for those seven attributes, the US-born respondents had an average mean score of 8.84. Among Russian respondents, the composite score was significantly higher, while it fell short among those born in three Asian cultures.

However, after we adjust the data to account for different uses of the scales, we find that Japanese and Korean samples have about the same satisfaction levels as the US-born sample. (The scores were adjusted to reflect the scale usage of the US-born sample; however, all scores could have just as easily been adjusted to reflect the scale usage of any of the cultures examined.) The Russian-born sample is still more satisfied, but not by the margin that was initially computed. Similarly, the Mandarin sample remains the least satisfied, but by a much smaller margin than initially suggested.

What if you prefer the top two box technique of comparing results? How does the use of the scale differ across various cultures? The accompanying volume provides a detailed explanation for how to adjust the data so that the results are comparable across these cultures.

The particular case of Japan

Just as Hispanic cultures tend to use the upper end of the scale more than other parts of the world, some Asian cultures use the upper end of the scale less often than other cultures do. Nowhere have I seen this more pronounced than among Japanese respondents. This comes up virtually every time I have conducted scaled research in Japan.

For example, I recently conducted research among members of a global nonprofit organization. The question was, "Please rate the extent of your agreement with the following statement: Based upon my understanding of them, I fully support and am committed to (the organization's) purpose, goals and objectives." There were six response options: strongly disagree, disagree, somewhat disagree, somewhat agree, agree and strongly agree.

Exhibit 6.2 Response profiles (total versus Japan)

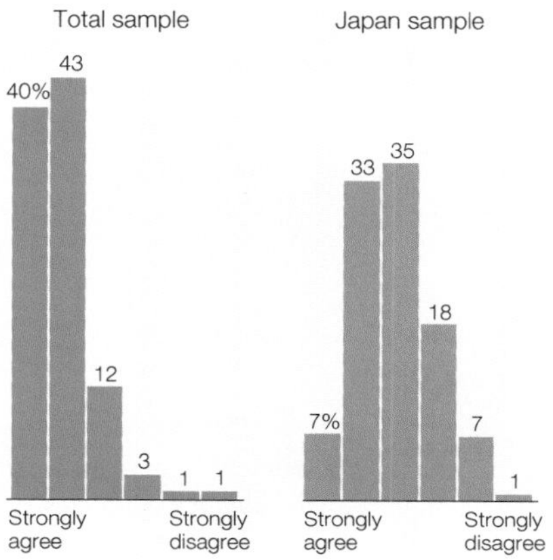

Exhibit 6.2 shows the response profile for the entire global sample of almost 11,000 respondents (including 423 Japanese respondents). It's worth noting that the organization is very strong in Japan, so there was no reason to believe that the Japanese profile should differ from that of other countries.

Statistically, there's no possibility that these two profiles came from the same population. But the difference is not because Japanese members of the organization are less committed to the goals of the organization; it's because they're culturally more reluctant to use the top response category.

Exhibit 6.3 Response profiles with adjusted Japanese profiles

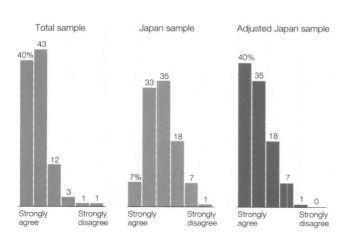

Exhibit 6.3 reveals what happens to the Japanese profile when we simply bump up each respondent's answer by one category (i.e., every 1 becomes a 2, every 2 becomes a 3, and so on until we merge the 5s and 6s). While this may seem like we're cheating somehow, this is actually a very legitimate adjustment process. We've fully maintained the differences in responses among the Japanese respondents (except the 5s and 6s), while at the same time converted the representation of those responses to a scale-usage that corresponds to most others around the world. The application of this simple adjustment makes the data much more useful if you're trying to conduct comparisons across cultures or across countries.

Summary
Research from individuals in different countries can be misleading in that some cultures use scales differently than others. Yet very few global brand tracking programs adequately account for this phenomenon.

Depending on how you're planning to use the results of global research, you may wish to use adjustment factors such as those suggested in this chapter to make the scores comparable across cultures. This is particularly relevant to research that will affect contingent compensation of managers (e.g., bonuses based on customer satisfaction measurements), along with customer service improvement initiatives, likely adoption of new products and others. In the absence of such adjustments, you may be unfair in your compensation programs or focus on the wrong geographical areas in developing brand or service improvement initiatives. The bottom line: if the objective of the research is to examine differences across cultures or regions, make sure the differences are real.

Questions to discuss with your research professionals
+ As a global company, have we considered the cultural differences among countries in our research?
+ How are we aggregating and reporting our research results by country or region?
+ Have we examined our brand research results to see if we're encountering the types of issues described in this chapter?
+ Are we adjusting for the different use of scales by some cultures? If not, why not?

Chapter 7
Segregating the Perceptions of Customers and Non-Customers

One of the most valuable benefits of brand research is learning how various audiences perceive different brands. To accomplish this, researchers usually ask survey respondents to rate different brands on a series of attributes, such as those described in Chapter 4. The results then can be used to construct a **Composite Brand Scorecard** that presents perceptions of each brand from the entire market—including both customers and non-customers. An example of a partial Composite Brand Scorecard from a computer security software environment is shown in Exhibit 7.1. (Note: I usually populate the scorecard with mean attribute ratings. The scores in Exhibit 7.1 were multiplied by 10 to mirror a 100-point maximum instead of a 10-point maximum.) This scorecard tells us which brand decision makers perceive as "best in class" in the marketplace. For example, the scorecard shows that Brand C is perceived as offering the more complete solution ("offers a total security solution"), but Brand A is seen as doing a better job of protection ("protects what I value"). This scorecard provides significant insight into the competitive strengths of individual brands and is critical in determining the optimal positioning for a brand.

> A Composite Brand Scorecard is extremely useful in assessing brands, yet its real value comes in developing separate scorecards for customers and for prospects. To assess your exposure to potential attrition, you need to understand how your customers see your brand on the same attributes they are seeing other brands for which they are not customers.

Exhibit 7.1 Example of a Composite Brand Scorecard

Description	Brand A	Brand B	Brand C	Brand D
Focuses solely on security needs	51.3	58.1	51.1	56.1
Superior customer support & technical service	26.9	30.9	36.2	29.8
Offers a total security solution	42.3	55.7	**61.6**	52.6
Helps me understand security risks	56.4	52.8	59.3	52.6
Protects me from a threat before it impacts me	69.2	70.3	68.3	63.2
Provides an integrated solution	43.6	57.7	60.4	45.6
Reduces my fear of online threats	71.8	72.8	69.4	70.2
Increases my confidence while using technology	56.4	64.2	64.2	57.9
Can be trusted with my home PC security	80.8	76.4	78.0	68.4
Protects what I value	**74.4**	67.5	67.9	63.2

Before I go any further, I want to offer a strong recommendation here: when you're compiling Composite Brand Scorecards, **do not include the perceptions of individuals who do not classify themselves as being at least somewhat familiar with the brand being rated.** This is consistent with the "gating chart" of the second chapter (shown in Exhibit 2.1), in which those not familiar with the brand are lost at Gate 2 and don't factor into the attribute ratings that drive the decisions made at Gates 3 and 4.

In fact, my research has consistently shown that respondents who are not at least somewhat familiar with the brand either provide a lot of "neutral" scores—e.g., 5s, which actually damage the mean scores that normally run in the range of 6.5 to 8.0—or they leave a lot of the attributes unrated because they aren't sufficiently familiar with the brand to rate them. In short, the opinions of these people simply don't matter as much, and they cloud the results from respondents whose opinions are more insightful.

As I mentioned above, the Composite Brand Scorecard is very useful because it provides insight into each brand's competitive strengths. If you're attempting to build a compelling promise or positioning for your brand, this is the first indication of the types of attributes you can build into that promise with the assurance that decision makers will find those attributes credible.

What you don't know at this point is whether those competitive strengths have any value in the eyes of decision makers—that is, whether they represent brand equities. (Remember that I am defining equities as the competitive advantages of a brand that decision makers find compelling.) Your brand may be far and away the best-in-class brand on an attribute that has essentially no relevance whatsoever to decision makers. Identifying which attributes "matter" and which do not is covered in depth later on in this book.

While the Composite Brand Scorecard is extremely useful, you can increase its value significantly by breaking it down into three subcomponents:
1. A **Customer Brand Scorecard** that reflects the perceptions of your brand and its competitors only among *decision makers who actually use your brand.*
2. A **Paired Brand Scorecard** that shows the perceptions of your brand and a single competitor among *customers of that competitor.* You can only run these pairings if your sample includes enough of your competitors' customers to make the comparison valid. However, you should run it for every competitor where the sample base is big enough.
3. A **Prospect Brand Scorecard** that reflects perceptions of your brand among *decision makers who are familiar with your brand but do not currently use it.*

Customer Brand Scorecard

This scorecard shows the perceptions of your brand and its competitors only among decision makers who actually use your brand. All three of the scorecards in this chapter—including this one—present perceptions of brands on high-level "acquisition" attributes (i.e., attributes that both customers and prospects of a brand could rate). You may wonder why you need to care about acquisition attributes for people who are already your customers.

Recall the point we addressed earlier: unless you're dealing with a customer who's new to the category, or you're operating in a multiple brand usage environment, **one brand's acquisition is another brand's attrition.** For the most part, customers are a zero-sum game. To evaluate the possibility of your customers switching to a competitor, you need to understand how they see you on the same attributes they see your competitors.

The Customer Brand Scorecard is a useful retention tool for this reason— it reveals where your brand is most vulnerable to the offerings of competitors in your category.

Paired Brand Scorecard

The Paired Brand Scorecard shows the perceptions of your brand and those of a single competitor among that competitor's customers. Paired brand scorecards are valuable from an acquisition standpoint. In a sense, they offer the converse view of the first scorecard. That is, they show where your competitors are vulnerable. Important attributes for which respondents perceive your brand as being stronger than—or as strong as—the competitors represent potential opportunities. These are themes you can leverage in your attempts to win those customers away.

Prospect Brand Scorecard

Finally, the Prospect Brand Scorecard reveals how non-customers (people who are familiar with your brand but do not currently choose it) perceive your brand. In essence, this scorecard looks at the message that your brand communicates to the world, based on your advertising, word-of-mouth, interpretations of the brand names you use and so on. It provides a benchmark that you can use to evaluate the effectiveness of these communication initiatives.

The performance of your brand on the first scorecard (which assesses your current customers) and the Prospect Brand Scorecard (which assess non-customers) reveals important aspects of your company's or product's performance, particularly if there are large gaps between the two. The Customer Brand Scorecard portrays the brand experience through the eyes of those who have actually experienced it, warts and all, while the Prospect Brand Scorecard portrays the communicated brand.

If these two scorecards align with a minimal gap between the two, that likely means the brand is delivering the experience that it is perceived as promising. The perceptions of both audiences match.

More troubling are the instances where there are large gaps between the two, meaning that perceptions of the brand do not line up with the actual experiences of customers. These can stem from at least two explanations:

+ First, the brand is doing a great job of exceeding expectations through the brand experience, yet this message hasn't made it to non-customers, either directly or through word-of-mouth.
+ Second, through negative advertising by a competitor, a lack of communication on your part or another reason, prospects believe that your brand is weak in areas where it's actually strong.

In rare occurrences, companies encounter a third situation, in which prospects' perceptions actually exceed those of customers. These cases need to be examined closely; sometimes they represent a flashing red warning sign. They indicate that the brand is failing to meet customer expectations. If this applies to critical attributes that drive brand preference, you'll need to fix the problems quickly. Word-of-mouth in these situations can do lasting damage to the brand.

Finally, if you extend the Prospect Brand Scorecard to include the perceptions of each competitor—again, only including decision makers who are not customers of that brand—you can gain considerable insight into who's winning the communications battle. This extended Prospect Brand Scorecard will identify the brands that are successfully building the perception of excellence on a given attribute in the absence of any firsthand experience with that brand.

The incumbent's advantage

Once you examine these various brand scorecards, you will very likely observe that the "incumbent" (i.e., the brand that a decision maker is currently using) has a significant advantage. That is, retention has an inherent advantage over acquisition. This is one reason why it costs so much more to acquire a new customer than to retain a current one.

There are several reasons for this advantage. First, as the laws of physics dictate, an object at rest tends to remain at rest until a sufficiently strong force is applied to it. This inertia applies to brand relationships as well—people usually don't like to change. Many decision makers remain reluctant to switch brands even when they're dissatisfied with their current choice. In some cases, particularly in the business-to-business environment, this is because there's a monetary cost to switching (e.g., contracts with penalty clauses, disruption from changing systems or processes, etc.). In other cases it may simply be loyalty, or a general skepticism about the category (i.e., "the devil you know is better than the devil you don't").

> In evaluating brand scores on various attributes, keep in mind that the incumbent brand holds a significant advantage—much like elections. My research consistently shows that a brand that is not used gives up between 0.5 and 1.0 points (on a 10-point scale) to a brand that is used.

A second advantage that accrues to the incumbent is that decision makers consistently rate the brands they use higher than brands they don't use. One might argue that this is simply decision makers justifying their choices— "Why would I use a brand that I think is inferior to others?" But the more likely explanation is that the actual experience with a brand provides proof of its capabilities, while assessments of other brands include natural skepticism or uncertainty, which lowers overall perceptions of those brands in the minds of non-customers.

My research has consistently found that brand incumbency is worth between half a point and a full point on a 10-point scale. This means that when you're trying to capture another brand's customer, you start about 0.7 points behind in a contest in which the "winning score" is usually around 7.5–8.0. It's a significant disadvantage.

Exhibit 7.2 profiles the differences in customer and non-customer perceptions across 40 different attributes relating to car rentals when one is out-of-town for personal reasons (e.g., on vacation). Among the eight leading brands, the mean difference between customers' perceptions of the brand and non-customers' perceptions of the same brand ranges from 0.40 to 1.15 points. For the entire group, the mean difference is 0.72 points.

The pattern shown below is the norm, not the exception. In environ-

Exhibit 7.2 Differences in perceptions of customers and prospects

Brand	Mean difference	Standard deviation
1	0.55	0.32
2	0.78	0.26
3	0.60	0.21
4	1.15	0.31
5	0.97	0.26
6	0.40	0.23
7	0.63	0.38
8	0.68	0.32
Composite	0.72	0.37

ment after environment, I've seen this pattern of brand usage being worth between a half point and a point, compared with brands that aren't being used. This applies both domestically and internationally. For example, averaging differences across 40 attributes and five brands in a telecommunications environment in Taiwan, the mean difference was 0.55 points, ranging from 0.34 points to 0.99 points.

Summary
Brand research can be very expensive. Make sure you derive the full value of that information. Composite Brand Scorecards can provide a multitude of insights into the relative perceptions of your brand and its competitors in the marketplace. As long as the sample sizes are sufficient, you should create brand scorecards for all three subgroups within the total respondent base: 1) the perceptions of all brands in the category among your current customers; 2) how your brand stacks up to competitors' in the eyes of their customers and 3) the perceptions of your brand among non-customers. These comparisons can provide distinct insights that many brand researchers often overlook.

Questions to discuss with your research professionals
+ Is our brand research designed in such a way that we can compute the various brand scorecards described in this chapter?
+ Is the sample large enough?
+ Do we have enough brand ratings for our key competitors?
+ Are we currently constructing a Customer Brand Scorecard?
+ Are we currently constructing a Paired Brand Scorecard?
+ Are we currently constructing a Prospect Brand Scorecard?
+ When we set improvement goals, are we considering the incumbent's advantage?

Chapter 8
Derived Brand Scorecards

Since customer perceptions tend to be higher than non-customer perceptions on a given attribute, brands with higher market shares usually enjoy an advantage on the Composite Brand Scorecard. That is, the Composite Brand Scorecard favors the brand with the greatest ratio of customers to non-customers. While this is realistic—the category leader usually is seen as better than other brands on most attributes—it's also misleading and could make the category leaders complacent about their brands' reputations.

> **Since customers tend to provide higher ratings for a brand than do non-customers, this artificially inflates the scores of brands with higher market shares. If you want to compare brand perceptions without the biasing influence of market share, construct a Derived Brand Scorecard.**

That's not the only bias you have to contend with, however. My research over the years has consistently shown that respondents who claim to be very familiar with a brand usually rate it higher than people who are only somewhat familiar with the brand. This is more than simply a restatement of incumbent advantage in that it occurs with both customers and non-customers. Among both groups, respondents who consider themselves very familiar with the brand usually provide higher ratings than do those who are only somewhat familiar with it.

As you can imagine, these two effects compound each other. Respondents who are both customers of a brand and very familiar with it tend to provide ratings that are 5 to 8 percent higher than the average rating for that brand. Non-customers who are only somewhat familiar with the brand are the lowest raters, providing scores that are on average about 5 to 8 percent lower than the total sample. The other two subgroups—customers who aren't very familiar with the brand, and non-customers who are—provide ratings that are closer to the overall sample. (I've observed the same pattern in other countries, though the spread is somewhat smaller in Asia.)

These effects can significantly skew your results, so you may want to

Exhibit 8.1 Best-in-class attributes, by brand of rental car

Brand X	Brand Y	All other brands
22 attributes	16 attributes	2 attributes

Exhibit 8.2 Two methods for determining the number of best-in-class attributes

Using actual brand scores

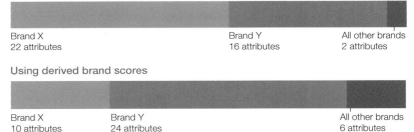

Brand X	Brand Y	All other brands
22 attributes	16 attributes	2 attributes

Using derived brand scores

Brand X	Brand Y	All other brands
10 attributes	24 attributes	6 attributes

adjust for them by creating something I call a **Derived Brand Scorecard**. The process requires removing the influence of the customer to non-customer ratio and brand familiarity in the Composite Brand Scorecard, so that you can assess the brands on an apples-to-apples basis. The resulting scores are called derived scores because they don't represent the actual scores for any of the brands. Instead, they're "artificial" scores derived from the Customer and Prospect Brand Scorecards.

If you don't account for these factors, you can be misled regarding which brands really are best in class. Consider the previously mentioned case of a study conducted in the rental car business (out-of-town for personal reasons). The original Composite Brand Scorecard showed that two brands dominated the best-in-class ratings among the 40 attributes that the study measured (Exhibit 8.1). Not surprisingly, these two brands enjoyed the highest share of the market, with Brand X somewhat ahead of Brand Y.

To understand if Brand X's dominance was due to its actual performance on the 40 attributes or if it was instead due to the effects of market share advantage and familiarity, we constructed a Derived Brand Scorecard. For each brand, we determined how many respondents were in each of the four possible categories: customers who were very familiar with it, non-customers who were very familiar with it, customers who didn't know the brand as well and non-customers who didn't know the brand as well.

Next we recomputed the scores for all 40 attributes, weighting the data to mirror an environment in which every company had the same brand relationship profile—meaning the same proportion of respondents in all four of those categories. The results are shown in Exhibit 8.2.

As you can see, this correction flips the findings, and puts Brand Y significantly ahead of Brand X. In fact, if Brand Y were to invest in increasing its brand awareness and familiarity to put it on a par with Brand X, it would take over leadership on 24 of the 40 attributes, leading it to become the preeminent brand in the market. This was important information for the management of Brand X to understand so that they could anticipate the risk of such measures by Brand Y.

Derived Benchmarks

This principle of using derived scores to adjust for certain biases doesn't apply just to Brand Scorecards. You can apply it to customer satisfaction research as well. Chapter 6 described a method that used both semantic scales and Likert scales to remove cultural biases in the way that respondents from different countries apply the scales. While this process is rigorous and highly valuable, it can also be very costly as you need large samples to compute the adjustment factors. Instead, researchers can apply the concepts of Derived Brand Scorecards to calibrate responses in a way that essentially eliminates cultural or segment bias. This technique is particularly useful in customer satisfaction research that compares different units (e.g., bank branches, retail stores, geographical regions).

Comparing satisfaction across different units sounds like an easy task: just survey customer satisfaction using a sound sampling plan and sufficiently large samples to develop reliable estimates of satisfaction. But the task is not this simple. Why not? Some demographic segments either use the satisfaction scale differently, or they're simply easier to satisfy than other customers. For example, older customers provide significantly higher satisfaction scores than other customers. On the flip side, male professionals are extremely tough raters. Either they're harder to satisfy or—again—they just use the scale differently.

The issue comes down to this: should bank managers or retail store managers with a higher proportion of "easy to please" customers be rewarded at the expense of managers whose customer portfolio is disproportionately "hard to please" individuals?

We can use the Derived Brand Scorecard technique to cancel out this effect, creating what I call a **Derived Benchmark**. The Derived Benchmark serves as a baseline for specific customer profiles against which individual brands or locations can be compared for a more accurate assessment of their performance.

As an example, suppose the mean satisfaction score for a particular branch (using a 10-point Likert satisfaction scale) is 6.81, compared with a system-wide mean of 7.35. Under most contingent compensation schemes, the manager of this branch would receive a lower-than-average rating for that component—and a lower bonus. However, now suppose that the expected

Some demographic segments either apply scales differently, or they're easier to satisfy than other customers. Customer satisfaction research has to account for these biases, particularly in comparing different units such as bank branches, retail stores or geographic regions.

satisfaction score for a branch with the specific demographic makeup of the example branch was 6.68. In this case, the example branch is actually performing almost 2 percent above average. In reality, this manager deserves an average or above average contribution—and a bigger bonus.

I describe the actual procedure behind Derived Benchmarks in more detail in *Fact-Based Branding in the Real World: A Simple Survival Guide for Research Professionals*. But in essence, this technique estimates the "expected performance" for a particular branch or location by reweighting the total sample results to reflect the demographic profile of the branch's or location's customers. Say that 20 percent of the customers at a particular branch or location are under age 25, another 35 percent are 25–49 and the remaining 45 percent are age 50 or older. We can estimate the expected satisfaction of the location's customers by weighting the total sample to reflect that demographic profile. The catch is that you need to have sufficient samples of each subgroup (e.g., under 25) to make the estimates reliable.

This procedure can be replicated for each branch, store, region or any other unit you want to analyze. Once you identify the key characteristics that you want to control—such as age, gender, culture and so on—you can determine what the scorecard for any unit should look like.

Summary
Derived Scorecards allow you to compare perceptions of one brand to those of another in a consistent manner. These scorecards level the playing field by removing the inherent advantage that the market leader has because the marketplace is more familiar with that brand. Derived Scorecards provide a better assessment of which brand is really best in class on a given attribute. In addition, the same technique can be used in your customer satisfaction measurements to develop Derived Benchmarks for various units, such as stores, locations, regions, etc.

Questions to discuss with your research professionals
+ How does our brand compare with our competitors' brands when we standardize the ratio of customers to non-customers?
+ Which brands are best in class on which attributes under these conditions?
+ Does our organization need to consider devoting resources to increasing awareness and familiarity?
+ Could we use Derived Benchmarks in our customer satisfaction research?
+ Have we looked at ratings from different groups of individuals to see if they use the rating scale differently?
+ What characteristics should we use to construct Derived Benchmarks?

Chapter 9
A Discussion of Statistical Significance

Statistical significance is one of the most used—and least understood—phrases in social research. An executive will often ask me, "Are the results statistically significant?" or "Is the survey statistically significant?" I think what the person really wants to know is, "Can I trust the results?"

Why should a CMO, or anyone else for that matter, care about statistical significance? What does it mean anyway? This is an important topic, and it comes up in just about every research project. Statistical significance is also a bit complex, so it's worth delving into here—just a little. I realize most CMOs and brand managers aren't statisticians, and I've tried to keep this volume reasonably free of technical jargon and formulas. However, on this topic I would ask that you tolerate some measure of technical detail. I hope that after finishing the chapter (and perhaps downing an aspirin or two), you'll feel more comfortable with the concept of statistical significance and reliability.

With that out of the way, statistical significance is really about the reliability of an estimate (e.g., a mean, a percentage and so on). If you want to understand how your customers feel about some aspect of your brand, theoretically you could interview every single one of them. Because that approach isn't really feasible, surveys instead typically look at some smaller subset of the population under consideration—a sample—under the theory that the perceptions of the subset can accurately represent those of the entire group. Because you're not actually talking to every single customer, however, survey results are subject to error (referred to as sampling error). This is because the results from one sample can sometimes differ from those of another, even if the two samples are the same size.

> Statistical significance looks at the reliability of an estimate mean or percentage. It tells you how confident you can be that the results of a sample truly line up with the results you would have obtained if you had talked to everyone in the universe under consideration.

Statistical significance or statistical reliability is about the degree of confidence you can have that the survey results from a sample are sufficiently close to the results you would have gotten if you'd talked to every possible respondent. You want to be confident you didn't get a "bad" sample.

One of the easiest ways to increase your confidence in sample results is to increase the size of the sample. As the sample size increases, the sampling error tends to decrease.

For example, suppose you wanted to find out if a coin is "fair" (i.e., equally likely to come up heads or tails when you flip it). The standard way to do this is to flip the coin a number of times and calculate the percentage of times it landed on heads. If the observed percentage is pretty close to 50, you'd conclude that the coin is fair. If the observed percentage is very different from 50, you might think that the coin isn't fair. But what's a reasonable difference? Put another way, how far does the percentage have to be from 50 before you can conclude with a high degree of confidence that the coin's unfair? And how many times do you have to flip it to figure this out?

Let's start with a single coin flip. You can either get a head or a tail. Even if the coin is perfectly fair, you cannot get anywhere close to the "correct" percentage of 50. With a single flip, the percentage of times the coin landed on heads is either 100 or zero. Those are "bad" results—the sample is too small, and the results are far from what we'd expect.

Now increase your sample—the number of flips—to two. At this point, there are four possible results: two heads (100 percent heads); a head and a tail, in either order (50 percent heads) and two tails (0 percent heads). The odds of getting a "bad" result are now cut in half. As you flip the coin more and more times, the observed percentages of heads will get closer and closer to 50 if the coin is fair.

Normal distribution and sampling error

In fact, if you keep increasing the sample size and plot the results of all possible samples of this size for a fair coin, the plot will get closer and closer to the familiar normal distribution, or "bell curve." That makes sense on an intuitive level. For just about anything you can measure, you'll find some outliers, but most of the results fall close to the average result: the middle part of the curve.

Say you wanted to determine the average height of people in a given town. You could measure every one of them (again, not really feasible). You could measure a single person (not accurate, because the sample is too small). Or you could measure enough people so that the results began to look like the normal distribution pattern—that reassuring bell-shaped curve. At a certain point your sample would be big enough that you could stop measuring and be reasonably confident that your results accurately represented the entire town.

Because results tend to arrange themselves this way, we can use the normal distribution to estimate how reliable a sample estimate is. The math behind this is actually pretty interesting (seriously).

Here's a political example. Suppose you were trying to predict who was going to win an election: Candidate A versus Candidate B. To do this, you survey a representative sample of 100 people who plan to vote. The sampling error for a percentage is really easy to calculate—you can do it with a drugstore calculator. The formula is simply:

Sampling Error $= \sqrt{p \cdot (100 - p) / n}$, where p is the percentage observed in the sample (e.g., if we observe a value of 45%, then p = 45) and n is the sample size (i.e., number of people in the sample).

To put in some actual numbers, suppose that 42 of the survey respondents say they're going to vote for Candidate A instead of Candidate B. (Assume all 100 people will vote, and they only have two options.) If 42 people say they'll vote for Candidate A, then p = 42. The sampling error would be the square root of (42 · 58 / 100) or 4.94.

This is where the normal distribution comes in. We saw above that the distribution of means of samples converges to the normal distribution as you increase the sample size. There's another concept to clarify here: standard deviation. In a normal bell curve, the standard deviation shows how spread out the results are, i.e., the thickness of the curve. Results with a small standard deviation are clustered around the mean, and if you plot those results, they look like a tall, thin candle. Results with a large standard deviation are more spread out—a plot of them looks like a low, rolling hill.

There's a way to calculate standard deviations (which I won't get into right now), but here's what you need to understand: one standard deviation away from the mean in either direction—i.e., greater than or less than the average—usually accounts for about two-thirds of the results (technically it's 68 percent). Two standard deviations from the mean account for about 95 percent of the results.

For a normal distribution with a mean of zero and a standard deviation of one—this is referred to as the standard normal distribution—95 percent of the results fall between −1.96 and +1.96. That number—1.96—comes up all the time in sampling research because it's used to calculate the 95 percent confidence interval. For the political example above, recall that our sampling error was 4.94. If we multiply that by 1.96, we get 9.67. As a result, we can be 95 percent confident that the "true" percentage that will vote for Candidate A is somewhere between 42 − 9.67 and 42 + 9.67 (or 32.33 and 51.67). Since 50 falls in this interval, we cannot call the election in the favor of Candidate B with 95 percent confidence.

I threw you a curve ball there. I was talking about standard deviations, then I threw in the term sampling error. Standard deviation refers to the distribution of individual observations, e.g., individual heights, individual votes. Sampling error refers to the distribution of means or percentages. As we saw from the coin discussion, means have less variation than the individual values themselves. In fact, the sampling error (of a mean) equals the standard deviation (of the individual values) divided by the square root of the sample size. So, the sampling error from a sample of size 100 is one-tenth the size of the standard deviation of the population from which the sample was drawn.

The observed mean from a sample plus or minus two times the sampling error (actually it is 1.96 times the sampling error) represents the 95 percent confidence interval. This is because the mean of a sample will fall within the "true" mean (i.e., the mean that would result if everyone in the universe were interviewed) plus or minus 1.96 times the sampling error 95 percent of the time.

Again, however, if you increase the sample size, your results become more reliable. Suppose the estimate of 42 percent had come from a sample of 400 voters instead. Now the sampling error is much smaller—the square root of (42 · 58 / 400), or 2.47. This makes the 95 percent confidence interval smaller as well: 42 ± 4.84, or 37.16 to 46.84. Since every outcome in that interval is less that 50 percent, we can now call the election in Candidate B's favor with at least 95 percent confidence. The size of the sample made all the difference.

As you can see from this discussion, every estimated mean or percentage in a survey has its own sampling error depending on the magnitude of the estimate itself. As Exhibit 9.1 demonstrates, **the sampling error depends not only on the sample size, but the value of p itself.** This is why you cannot make a blanket statement about the "statistical significance" of an entire sample. Every estimate has its own level of sampling error.

For a sample of n = 400, if the observed percentage is 50, the 95 percent confidence interval is 45.1 to 54.9. That is, we're 95 percent confident that the actual percentage among the entire population is between 45.1 percent and 54.9 percent.

Exhibit 9.1 Confidence interval for sample sizes of 400 and 1,000

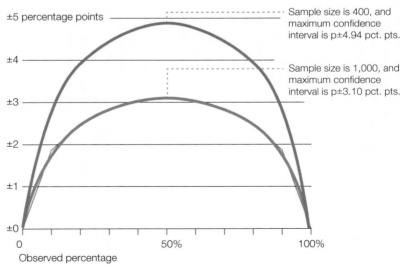

95% confidence interval for a percentage

±5 percentage points — Sample size is 400, and maximum confidence interval is p±4.94 pct. pts.

Sample size is 1,000, and maximum confidence interval is p±3.10 pct. pts.

Observed percentage

But look what happens if the observed percentage is 20 percent (p = 20). Now the 95 percent confidence interval is considerably smaller, between 16.08 percent and 23.92 percent.

A person responsible for research at a leading health care provider recently described the results presented in a report as "malfeasance" because some of the conclusions were based on samples of fewer than 100 observations. She based this statement on the fact that the sample wasn't large enough to present reliable findings. This revealed her lack of understanding of what it means for a result to be statistically significant. A small difference between the attribute ratings of two brands can be significant at the 90 percent or 95 percent confidence level if the sample is large enough, but a large difference can be significant at these same levels of confidence even if the samples are small. So beware thinking that you always have to have large samples to draw reliable conclusions. You just need to observe larger differences when you have smaller samples.

So what does this all mean in practical terms? What bearing does it have on designing a sample survey? The answer is that the **reliability of an estimate increases as the sample size increases.** If you're estimating a percentage, for example, you can be assured that the standard error of the estimate of the percentage (based on a simple random sample of the population) will be reliable within ±4.9 percentage points (5.0 if you use 2 instead of 1.96 as the multiplier) if you survey 400 people. This is why some people believe that a result won't be "statistically significant" if it's based on fewer than 400 observations.

Statistical significance of the difference between two percentages
Okay, just a little more detail before we wrap this up. If you're comparing the values of two percentages (i.e., trying to determine if the difference between two percentages is statistically significant), the formula gets a bit more com-plicated. This is because both percentages are subject to sampling variation. If the two percentages come from the same sample (e.g., all respondents rated both brands), then the formula for the standard error of the difference becomes approximately:

$$se = \sqrt{p \cdot (100 - p) / n}, \text{ where } p = (p_1 + p_2) / 2,$$

If the percentages are from independent samples, the formula becomes:

$$se = \sqrt{[p_1 \cdot (100 - p_1) / n_1] + [p_2 \cdot (100 - p_2) / n_2]}.$$

In general, comparing percentages from the same sample is more reliable. If you're using separate, independent samples of the same size, you essen-tially increase the standard error by a factor of 1.4 since both samples produce sampling errors.

This entire chapter thus far has dealt with percentages, but if you're comparing two means, or differences of means, things get quite complicated. You can no longer calculate the standard error simply. The values of $p \cdot (100 - p)$ in the equations above now get replaced by s^2, where s is the standard deviation observed in the sample. This value is a standard output of statistical programs like SPSS or SAS.

Summary

As a CMO or brand manager, it's important to understand what statistical significance means. You cannot make a blanket statement that defines the "statistical significance" of a survey. Some people tend to dismiss significant information if they don't think the sample size is large enough, or—equally incorrect—they accept findings as significant just because the sample size exceeded some rule-of-thumb threshold. In fact, every estimate has its own level of statistical reliability, and that varies based on both the sample size and the specific responses you observe.

Sample sizes of 400 or 1,000 are often used because they ensure maximum confidence intervals for a percentage of ± 5 percentage points or ± 3 points, respectively. But these sample sizes don't have magical powers, and neither one ensures statistical significance of every estimate derived from the research.

Questions to discuss with your research professionals

+ What are the key estimates in our brand research that affect our business?
+ What are the sampling errors associated with those estimates?
+ Are the sampling errors small enough that we don't need to be concerned, or do we need to increase our sample sizes?
+ What are the key differences in estimates that we track and report?
+ At what level of confidence are these differences statistically significant?

Discovering the compelling truth of a brand

This section explains how you can determine the most important competitive strengths of your brand—the ones you need to consistently communicate in your messaging—and which gaps with competitors are most critical to close. I also discuss various statistical modeling techniques, along with some tips for what to do when respondents don't answer survey questions. Finally, a couple of case studies reveal how brand research can inform business strategy as well.

Chapter 10
Compelling Truth and Identifying Brand Attributes That Matter

Scott Lerman, CEO of Lucid Brands, coined the phrase "compelling truth" in a branding context when he was president of the New York office of branding firm Enterprise IG (now The Brand Union). The term so simply and elegantly describes the Holy Grail for any CMO, brand manager or brand researcher: what's true about a brand that compels people to buy it or use it? Whatever that truth is, that's the message the brand should be communicating again and again in the marketplace.

Do you understand the compelling truth of your brand? How do you know? If you're basing that conclusion on the stated importance of attributes from customers you've surveyed, you may be making very bad brand decisions. Potentially worse, are you competing with other brands simply by trying to close the largest gaps? If any aspect of brand management absolutely requires the use of fact-based research techniques, it's understanding the compelling truth of your brand.

Let's focus on the "truth" part first. To succeed, a brand's promise must be true, both in reality and in the eyes of those who influence the purchasing decision. Note that these are two different elements. When it comes to purchase influencers, the phrase "perception is reality" applies. They must believe a brand's claims to be true. This element of compelling truth comes out in the competitive ratings provided in the brand scorecards that I described earlier.

The other half of truth is whether the claim is actually true, not just perceived to be true. As brand consultants, we use interviews with key executives in a company to determine which claims we can make and which would be contrary to the capabilities or "DNA" of the company or brand. It's important that a brand's promise be grounded in reality; my research has shown that the shelf life of "smoke and mirrors" in the brand world is at most 18 months. If a brand makes a claim that it cannot live up to, that house of cards will likely collapse within a year and a half.

> You need to identify what is both true and what is compelling about a brand to decision makers. Brand scorecards combined with head-to-head comparisons between brands provide crucial information.

Some years ago, a leading health insurer in Florida wanted to develop an optimal promise (i.e., positioning) for its brand. It used the techniques described in this book to identify the key drivers of brand preference for that category. The Composite Brand Scorecard revealed that one of this company's competitors was communicating the most important drivers perfectly. As a result, this smaller company was building share at a remarkable clip—a phenomenon that our client could not explain until they saw the research. Yet the claims made by this competitor were not actually true. Sure enough, within 18 months, that competitor crumbled, its share plummeted and it was ultimately acquired by another carrier.

Now let's turn to the second component of compelling truth: the "compelling" aspect. Here the challenge is to identify which brand attributes really matter to those who are influencing the purchase decision. The various brand score-cards allow you to identify the relative strengths of each brand among a defined set of competitors. However, this analysis gives no insight whatsoever into which of these competitive strengths actually are true brand equities (i.e., which ones significantly affect the purchasing decision). A brand may be best in class on several attributes, but if those attributes do not persuade people to buy the product, the wins are Pyrrhic victories at best. For example, some brands emphasize their long track record of success in a specific category. But if you don't know for sure that customers use that fact in choosing among competing brands, who cares? An advantage on an attribute that doesn't matter in the purchasing decision isn't really an equity at all.

One overused solution is to simply ask respondents to rate the importance of each attribute or to rank attributes in order of importance—two forms of "stated importance." The problem with this approach is that very few individuals really understand how they make decisions (or what attributes drive that decision). As mentioned in Chapter 2, when asked how they make choices, people tend to provide answers that make them appear savvy or "politically correct" (e.g., buying only brands that are environmentally responsible or organic). Others rate every attribute on the list as important. Over the years, my analyses of stated importance metrics have repeatedly shown that there's only a passing resemblance between the attributes that buyers claim to be important and their actual buying behavior. Many of the highest ranked attributes have little or no connection to the brands that people actually choose.

Statisticians used to debate whether stated importance or "derived" importance (determined indirectly from other data) is the better technique, but that argument has been put to rest—most statisticians now agree that derived techniques are superior. Unfortunately, this hasn't changed research methodology much. I recently saw an article stating that more than half of all surveys that evaluate importance still do so using stated methods. Perhaps this is because it's so easy to simply ask people to state the importance of specific attributes, or maybe it's because many researchers don't understand how to derive importance.

A simple way of deriving insights regarding the importance of an attribute is to correlate the attribute ratings with an outcome metric such as brand preference or brand favorability (or overall satisfaction, in the case of customer satisfaction research). While this provides useful insight, this method is also limited in its ability to understand the brand decision process.

In this context, the analysis evaluates a particular brand by itself, in a vacuum. This is artificial, in that it doesn't consider perceptions of any competing brands. People simply do not make brand decisions this way. Instead, they make them in a competitive environment, and the final choice usually comes down to a head-to-head comparison of two or three brands (i.e., the short list of options at Gate 4 of the decision making process).

You can get around this problem by extending the brand analyses from static to dynamic evaluations. That is, you ask respondents to indicate their preference for one brand versus another in a head-to-head setting. Researchers rarely use this elegant yet simple technique even though it offers much greater insight into the competitive dynamics of a particular product category. Individuals generally cannot accurately describe how they make brand choices, but they can express their preference for one brand over another with reasonable accuracy.

Rather than simply asking a decision maker to choose Brand A versus Brand B in a survey, I find it more useful to ask respondents to allocate a fixed number of points—or "chips"—between the two brands, to indicate their strength of preference. (This is called a Constant Sum Preference, or CSP, exercise.) It's a bit like being at the roulette table in a casino where bettors can put a certain number of chips on number 18 (Brand A) or number 25 (Brand B) depending on how strongly they feel that number will come up on the next spin of the wheel.

In addition, while you can use any number of chips, I strongly recommend an odd number, because it forces a respondent to choose one brand over the other. If you use an even number, respondents can put the same number of chips on each brand, which is a tie and tells you almost nothing. More specifically, I prefer to use 11 chips as the total in the CSP exercise. This allows the responses to spread out a bit and give you separation, without making the math too hard for the respondent. (If you go higher than 11—like 13, 15, 17, etc.—people have to work to figure out which pairs of numbers add up to the total. It sounds like simple arithmetic, but respondents are usually answering a lot of these questions at one sitting, and you need to keep things relatively simple or they won't provide usable information.)

By employing this technique, we now have indicators of preference for a series of brand pairs—Brand A vs. Brand B, Brand A vs. Brand C, Brand B vs. Brand C and so on. You can think of this as a surrogate measure for actually purchasing these brands. If the respondent were in a store, and Brand A and Brand B, were on the shelf in front of him, which one would he choose, and how strongly would he prefer it?

This technique lets you go beyond mere correlations of attributes with outcomes for a single brand. Instead, you can correlate **differences** in brand attribute ratings with **differences** in brand preference. This is a much more powerful way to measure the importance of an attribute because it links specific attributes to actual preferences.

In fact, I've found that this type of correlation analysis can often identify why the market leaders in a category sit in that position. If we were entering into a market with a new brand, this might be sufficient information to determine whether we wanted to proceed.

By itself, however, this analysis is only somewhat useful for a brand that's already out in the market. Existing brands have an image in the minds of decision makers. The key question for such brands is, "Given current perceptions of my brand in the marketplace, what aspects would yield the greatest incremental improvement in brand preference?"

In fact, for some attributes it's only important that you meet a minimum threshold. Think about the size of a bank. If you had just moved into a new community and the most convenient bank was a very small savings and loan or community bank, you might have concerns about its long-term existence. Will some mega-bank take it over in the next year or so? On the other hand, once you're convinced the bank is big enough, size no longer matters. Further increases in the size of the bank would not increase your preference for it— and at some point it might actually work against your preference.

Exhibit 10.1 shows the difference between a "threshold attribute" (Attribute one) that only matters up to a point and an attribute for which further improvements continue to win customers (Attribute two).

Exhibit 10.1 Differences in impact on brand preference

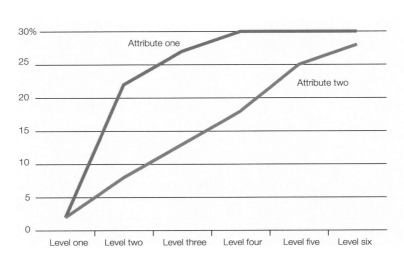

To identify how much different brand attributes affect brand preference on the margin, you'll likely have to use some form of brand preference modeling. This topic is discussed in Chapter 12.

Now, we can finally identify the compelling truth of our brand. The analysis of how much each attribute drives brand preference reveals what buyers find compelling (and even quantifies how compelling they find it). And the brand scorecards reveal the extent to which decision makers believe our brand actually delivers on those compelling attributes.

Summary

Before you develop marketing materials, ads or other brand communications, it's imperative that you understand the compelling truth of your brand. That is, you need to understand what attributes of a brand matter to decision makers and whether they think your brand has credibility in making claims on those attributes.

It's easy to get at the "truth" part. Individuals can rate the extent to which they believe various attributes describe brands. The "compelling" part is more difficult. You can't simply ask people what matters. Given the value of your brand as a corporate asset, it's likely to be worth it to invest in some advanced modeling techniques that will reveal how decisions are really made, not what people tell you. Then you can develop communications that will generate demand for your brand.

Questions to discuss with your research professionals
+ What do we know about the compelling truth of our brand?
+ How are we determining what's important to customers and prospects? Are we simply asking them?
+ If we're deriving importance, are we doing it in a vacuum or in a competitive context (e.g., through head-to-head comparisons with competing brands)?

Chapter 11
Buying Environments

To decipher how people make buying decisions, it's critical to keep in mind that buying takes place in a context. These contexts can vary significantly from one transaction to the next. For example, decisions that involve a lot of money (in a B2C setting) or involve mission-critical services (in a B2B setting) are made very differently from decisions regarding what brand of copier paper to purchase at Staples. Even decisions in the same category can differ depending on who is making them. The logistics manager purchasing a fleet of automobiles for a service company will not make decisions the same way as a couple of young parents purchasing their first car. To isolate these factors and better understand what truly drives brand preference, we need to define a buying context that contains homogeneous decision makers—that is, those who apply similar criteria for making brand choices.

There are at least three dimensions that define a homogeneous buying environment (i.e., a context in which brand decisions are fairly consistent across all the potential buyers in that context). They include:
+ the complexity of the product or service being purchased
+ the role of the person influencing or making the purchase
+ the geography in which the purchase takes place

1. Complexity of the product or service
Most people would agree that the decision as to which brand of breakfast cereal to purchase is very different from the decision regarding which brand of jet aircraft a company should purchase. The cereal decision is low-risk, in that there are few ramifications or costs if the choice is wrong. It's also simple—the primary food shopper within the household makes the choice unilaterally, or in some cases fulfills a request from another family member. On the other hand, the purchase of a corporate jet involves a high degree of risk and cost, and the decision is usually very complex. A committee within the company will likely spend a considerable period of time deliberating before it ultimately chooses which aircraft to purchase.

> To understand how buying decisions are made, we need to be sure that we're studying a homogeneous context. At a minimum, such a context should be defined by the type or category of the product or service, the role of the individual making the decision and the geography in which the purchase is being made. These three dimensions define unique "buying environments."

This complexity dimension is particularly important for corporate brands that have multiple lines of business (LOBs). The purchase process for commercial banking services, for example, is very different than that for investment banking, even though the same person (the CFO and/or CEO) may take the lead role in both decisions. These are complex services, but they have substantially different drivers of brand preference. Buyers of commercial banking services tend to look for a conservative institution that has mastered executional excellence and has resolute integrity. On the other hand, buyers of investment banking services tend to look for an aggressive institution that will get them the best deal.

So how can the same company offer both commercial banking services and investment banking services? In the case of Citigroup, it used separate brands. For a period of time, Citigroup offered its commercial banking services under the Citibank brand and its investment banking services under the Salomon Smith Barney brand (until the latter brand was abandoned in 2003).

In contrast, when Bank of America and NationsBank merged, CEO Hugh McColl made it very clear that the various parts of the organization would "fight under one flag" (i.e., have the same name). As a result, the personality of the new Bank of America could be neither conservative nor aggressive. Instead, the bank was positioned around its ability, passion and willingness to make banking work in ways it never had before. The key in corporate banking for Bank of America was the role of the "relationship officer," a single individual who would truly understand the needs of each client and provide conservative commercial banking expertise or aggressive investment banking skills as appropriate.

2. Role of the person making or influencing the decision
The second dimension—the role of the person making the purchasing decision—is particularly relevant to business-to-business environments, which often involve committees. Consider the purchase of the mass spectrometer mentioned earlier in this book. The scientist who will actually use the piece of equipment would employ very different buying criteria than the purchasing agent. The scientist is more likely to consider usability, accuracy and other product features, while the purchasing agent is typically more concerned with the cost, along with service and warranty considerations.

3. Geography in which the purchase decision takes place
My research has repeatedly shown that decisions for the same type of product can differ significantly in different regions of the world. For example, the criteria used for the purchase of heavy construction equipment in Europe differ significantly from those used in the United States, due to the different market structure and greater reliance on dealers in the US. In Asia, the purchase process for many, if not most, products or services, tends to put more weight on globally recognized and respected brands. Brands that are neither global leaders nor local, lower priced alternatives often struggle.

Putting it all together

The reason the buying environment is so important is that if we mix fundamentally different decision criteria, we may get a result that is totally meaningless. If you include both the scientist and the purchasing agent in a single sample, their counteracting influences may prevent you from identifying either cost or performance as a key driver of brand preference.

Hence, in designing a sampling or analysis plan, it's critical to specify the buying environment. Separating multiple environments and studying them individually is often more expensive from a data collection standpoint. But simply lumping them together may be more costly in the long run, as you may misidentify—or miss entirely—the key drivers of brand preference.

In this chapter I've restricted the description of a buying environment to just three dimensions. However, additional (or different) dimensions may apply in specific circumstances. For example, in the case of corporate banking, the size of the client company matters. Large companies tend to have strong financial expertise in-house, and when they hire a corporate banker, they're often looking for consistent execution. On the other hand, middle market firms often need value-added expertise beyond merely executing transactions. In many cases, mid-sized firms still operate like small businesses, and as a result they need more involved corporate banking services.

Without controlling for that dimension, conducting market research into the preferences of corporate banking clients could be meaningless. Other buying environments may look at other critical dimensions. This topic merits considerable thought before launching into brand measurements and/or modeling.

Summary

Even if you're using rigorous fact-based branding tools, you may fail to recognize critical aspects of the purchase process if you don't pay careful attention to certain aspects of the research design. Ensure that you're not comparing the buying process for products and services that are very different in price and/or complexity. And don't blend the perceptions and preferences of different buyers, such as purchasing agents and end users. When you derive results from a homogeneous buying environment, you should have very powerful data on your hands. When you blend buying environments, all that power may be lost.

Questions to discuss with your research professionals
+ What is the makeup of the respondent bases in our brand research studies?
+ In identifying the attributes that matter to decision makers, are we sure we're analyzing the data from homogeneous buying environments? That is, can we reasonably believe that all the people in the data set would use similar criteria for making buying decisions?
+ Are our data sets large enough that we could do some testing to see if different groups of decision makers are applying similar value structures?
+ If not, what would it cost to change our research design to allow this?

Chapter 12
Modeling Brand Preference to Determine Business Impact

As I've mentioned previously in this book, people don't tend to make decisions about brands on a conscious level. This is why they often have so much difficulty in accurately describing the reasons behind their choices. In this chapter, we'll talk about identifying the subconscious scorecard that decision makers use in making a brand choice.

Much of the statistical modeling done in the past—as well as much of that done today—is in the form of a "macro-model." In this approach, researchers analyze the results from an entire sample of data and construct the model as if it applied equally to all decision makers; hence the use of the term "macro." To oversimplify things a bit, it's as if researchers were to bunch everyone's survey responses together and then predict that customers behave according to the average response.

> Statistical techniques such as regression analysis are examples of "macro-modeling" techniques. They are based on the total sample and assume all buyers are the same. Micro-models, which acknowledge that different decision makers may have different consideration sets, can be much more powerful in simulating market responses to brand initiatives.

Regression analysis is an example of macro-modeling. It determines a linear relationship between a dependent variable and a series of independent variables. For example, if you wanted to predict daily sales for an ice cream truck (the dependent variable), you would look at a couple of different factors, such as the weather, the location of the truck and whether school was in session (independent variables). Regression analysis can tell you how much each of these factors is likely to drive sales for a given day. But it's a macro-model, because it assumes all buyers are the same. What about the potential buyer who isn't in school? What about buyers who want ice cream in any weather? Your regression model won't fit their buying habits very well.

In contrast, a "micro-model" attempts to explain the variation of a dependent variable at the level of individual respondents. A micro-model acknowledges that if you change the perceptions of a given brand attribute, that will have a different impact on one decision maker than it has on another. Part of this is because different decision makers may include different sets of brands in their consideration set, or short list of potential options.

As a simple example, consider three people seeking to buy a car in the same category (i.e., a homogeneous buying environment). One person is sufficiently familiar with Toyota, Honda, Nissan and Buick to include them in her consideration set. The second person is considering Toyota and Saab. The third person is considering VW, Saab and Volvo. A shift in perceptions of Toyota would have no effect on the third buyer (who isn't familiar with the brand). Also, it likely would have a greater effect on the second buyer than the first, at least from the standpoint of the a priori odds that this person will ultimately buy a Toyota. Why? Toyota is up against three other brands with the first buyer, and only one with the second buyer.

This is the drawback of using a traditional macro-model in a single brand environment. It doesn't factor in the effects of perceptions of the brand's competitors. In any environment in which multiple brands are competing with each other—which is how the real world usually works—macro-models of this type tend to be diagnostic rather than predictive. That is, they help you understand which factors affect a brand's favorability or customer satisfaction, but they make poor predictions regarding brand preference.

In contrast, micro-models allow you to examine market dynamics in which competing brands interact. They consider all brands and allow different decision makers to have different consideration sets. When one brand gains share, micro-models identify the other brands that lose share. This ability to reflect the dynamic nature of markets makes micro-models very powerful in predicting shifts among brands.

Another benefit of this type of micro-model and its predictive capability is that it can be used to estimate the ROBI before you implement a specific branding initiative. As long as you can determine the financial return on incremental revenue increases and the likely costs required to achieve desired goals on specific attributes—both relatively easy to estimate—you can calculate the expected ROBI. This allows the traditional focus on brand alone (e.g., brand favorability, likelihood to purchase, etc.) to expand to include the economics of brand initiatives as well. Chapter 19 covers ROBI in more detail.

Finally, by being able to determine the economic benefit of improving a specific attribute relative to its cost, you can now focus resources and prioritize brand initiatives based on those likely to yield the greatest return, rather than simply trying to fix every gap the research reveals. You might find that consumers perceive a competitor as best in class on several attributes that the model reveals are completely unimportant in the buying decision. The appropriate response: let the other brand own those while you focus on other attributes that really matter.

The companion volume to this book, *Fact-Based Branding in the Real World: A Simple Survival Guide for Research Professionals*, presents a step-by-step discussion of how you can construct a powerful micro-model of the decision-making process. I've deliberately left out those details here, but I encourage readers who want more information to refer to that volume for a more in-depth discussion.

The fundamentals of the model were originally designed by some very smart people at Research International's Technical Services group in London. After that company stopped supporting the tool, I built a better version from scratch, using many of the same principles but improving its predictive capabilities. Today this integrated set of statistical applications—in one version or another—has been used in more than 1,000 client applications in over 70 countries around the world, and it has generated extremely accurate results according to several validation studies. In short, it's a very powerful tool.

A recent model I constructed using this approach was for a global professional services firm. The model used a sample of only 300 decision makers—100 in the US and 50 in each of four other countries. It predicted that increasing the key drivers of brand preference by specified amounts would lead to a share increase of 92 basis points, or 0.92 percentage points. Two years later, a brand tracking measurement revealed an actual share increase of 90 basis points, or 0.90 percentage points.

This is remarkable accuracy for a sample of that size. It demonstrates both the power of the model and how consistently people make decisions (despite their inability to explain how they made them). Perceptions of a brand may change reasonably rapidly, but—in the absence of a major paradigm shift, such as a disruptive new technology—the criteria that are used to make brand decisions tend to change very slowly. People's purchasing behavior is relatively engrained, and you can make accurate predictions based on that.

Once you've built the statistical model of decision making, it's relatively easy to construct a simulation model that reveals the impact of changes in a single attribute or a collection of attributes. The simulator allows you to play out "what-if" scenarios, both for changes in perceptions of your brand and for potential competitive responses. I use this simulation model to identify the leverage or business impact associated with each attribute. Those with relatively high impact are defined as the critical drivers of brand preference—the attributes that truly define what is compelling to decision makers in a given buying environment.

A comparison with other types of decision-making models
The micro-model described in this chapter is only one of many that are routinely used in brand research. Three additional types of models merit discussion: conjoint analysis, discrete choice models and structural equations models.

Conjoint analysis and **discrete choice models** are similar in that they both attempt to model decisions based on respondents' ranking or rating of various product or service bundles. Both techniques present respondents with bundles described through a set of factors, each of which has a defined set of levels. The levels can be ordinal, such as price, or they can also be categorical, such as brand (e.g., Audi, VW, Saab, Lexus, BMW, Mercedes-Benz).

Next, respondents are asked to sort alternative options by preference, to rate each set of options or to choose one alternative from each set. An example of a discrete choice exercise for choosing a gas station is shown in Exhibit 12.1. In its simplest form, a conjoint analysis exercise involves indicating preference for Option A versus Option B, then repeating this for several other pairs of options. With a "full profile" conjoint exercise, the respondent is exposed to every combination of factors and levels at least once. If there are too many combinations, one can use Adaptive Conjoint Analysis in which the process "learns" during the survey that certain levels of a factor are not desirable to particular respondents and doesn't include them in subsequent steps.

> Other types of models used in brand research include conjoint analysis, discrete choice modeling and structural equations modeling. A major difference between the type of micro-model discussed earlier and conjoint analysis or discrete choice modeling is that the latter options provide all the information a respondent needs, while the former relies on respondents' perceptions of a brand, even if those perceptions are incorrect. Buyers choose on perceptions of what they believe is true.

Discrete choice modeling differs from conjoint analysis primarily in that it allows respondents to choose from a variety of options at the same time, rather than just two, and it can include an option of not selecting any of the alternatives presented (i.e., "none of the above"). Both techniques use the

Exhibit 12.1 Example of a discrete choice exercise

Option A

Brand	Distance from home	Price of gas
Exxon	0.5 miles	$3.50 per gallon

Option B

Brand	Distance from home	Price of gas
Shell	1.0 miles	$3.40 per gallon

Option C

Brand	Distance from home	Price of gas
Mobil	0.8 miles	$3.30 per gallon

Option D

Brand	Distance from home	Price of gas
BP	0.2 miles	$3.80 per gallon

information derived from the comparisons to determine the relative value, or "utility," for each level of each factor. In that way, the utilities become a form of importance metric. In addition, both techniques include simulators that predict the likely uptake of alternative offerings in the marketplace.

So how do conjoint analysis and discrete choice modeling differ from the type of predictive micro-model described earlier? A fundamental difference is that conjoint analysis and discrete choice modeling fully inform the respondent of the features of the product or service so that the survey respondent fully understands the differences in the product or service bundles being evaluated. On the other hand, the micro-model described earlier is grounded in respondents' perceptions of a product, service or brand. Using the gas station example, this model would not tell the respondent the distance or gas price. Instead, it would ask the respondent to rate the extent to which they felt stations of each brand are convenient to their home and offer competitive pricing.

I know what you're thinking. Why look at perceptions instead of facts? Because, as the saying goes, in brand research "perception is reality." When consumers make a purchase, they base that choice on what they believe about the brand. (Think about it. Do you really drive around and measure the distance from your home and canvass all the different prices that day before you pull into a gas station, or do you make assumptions regarding convenience and relative pricing?) Whether those beliefs are true in reality doesn't really matter, especially at the time of purchase. The truth of those perceptions will factor in later on in the context of repeat purchases. But early on, it's simply not a primary concern of branding research. (Of course, if you are positioning and promoting your brand around attributes that are perceived to be true but really aren't, that can become a major problem.)

Nonetheless, while conjoint analysis and discrete choice modeling may be less than ideal for modeling brand preference, they're both powerful tools that are particularly useful in new product development where the objective is to determine what features might create greater demand or be seen as worth more than others.

Structural equations modeling (SEM) actually refers to a family of related procedures, rather than a single, specific technique. In general, however, SEM is a large-sample tool that tends to be confirmatory in nature. That is, rather than identifying a model, SEM takes the researcher's initial hypothesis and evaluates whether that model seems to fit the data.

Used primarily in epidemiology and social sciences research, SEM is a valuable tool in identifying and quantifying the effect one variable has on another. It allows for direct causal relationships where A directly affects B, and reciprocal relationships where A affects B and B, in turn, affects A. Because it quantifies these effects, SEM creates an importance metric that researchers can use to build predictive models.

A primary difference between SEM and the type of micro-model described in this chapter is that SEM is a static model. That is, SEM examines how attributes affect each other, but it doesn't examine how different brands are competing with each other in the marketplace. A researcher could potentially use SEM to identify the key relationships between individual attributes and the perceived "value" of a brand, but that would require additional modeling work to account for the fact that different decision makers include different brands in their consideration sets.

Summary

A decade or so ago, cross-tabs were still a big deal, but the techniques used to analyze brand data have become far more sophisticated since then. Nowadays, I rarely even produce cross-tabs for a client. Why would I—or why would any brand manager or CMO—settle for mundane, low-value analyses of brand data? Instead, fact-based branding techniques like predictive micro-models can provide you with information that is light years ahead of garden variety market research and cross-tabs. These tools can give you critical information about how decision makers make choices and how you should be communicating your brand.

In addition to predictive micro-models, the three models described in the latter part of this chapter can also help you derive significant value from data. Some of these tools are more relevant to new product development than to the management of existing brands, but any CMO, brand manager or research professional should at least become familiar with what each of these tools can and cannot do.

Questions to discuss with your research professionals

+ Can we build a micro-model of the decision process for our brand?
+ Can we simulate the effects of changes in perceptions of our brand—and/ or those of our competitors—on a single attribute or series of attributes?
+ Have we ever validated our models to see if they are reliable and predictive?
+ Have we looked into the variety of statistical models that might add value to our brand research?
+ What are we trying to do with these models (e.g., examine the viability/appeal of various features/benefits, identify the key drivers of brand preference, etc.)?
+ Are we using these models appropriately? Are we fully informing decision makers of choices rather than letting them make choices based on their perceptions of the various brands?
+ Should we try different approaches to see if we get the same results?

Chapter 13
How Fact-Based Branding Efforts Can Inform Business Strategy

The last few chapters have been fairly technical. At this point, I'd like to offer two case studies that show the ways these models can shed light on the buying process. The first is an examination of the financial services industry in the late 1990s. Even though that's more than a decade ago, the insights derived from that examination are still relevant to companies that have multiple lines of business and want to bundle those businesses into a single integrated offering. The second case study reveals how a simple brand evaluation commissioned by one of the nation's leading life insurance companies as a "checkup" transformed the way many life insurance businesses go to market today.

Case study 1: The challenge of being an integrated financial services provider

In the late 1990s, many of the world's largest banks were racing to become the leading "global integrated financial services provider." These banks wanted to successfully market a wide variety of financial products and services under a single, globally esteemed brand, including commercial banking, investment banking, retail banking, private banking, asset management, property and casualty insurance, and life insurance, among others. The banks assumed that a single, powerful brand could be the leader in all these diverse areas.

> This chapter takes a look at two case studies. The first shows how an understanding of the attributes that drive the purchase of financial products and services explained the failure of megabanks to become successful "global integrated financial services companies." The second study shows how a simple brand health exercise transformed the way many life insurance companies go to market today.

None of the major banks was ever particularly successful in achieving this goal. Why not? To understand what went wrong, we need to look at what drives the purchase process for these varying products and services.

I've spent much of my career conducting research for the financial services industry. Over that time, I used many of the tools described in this book to understand the key drivers of brand preference for a wide range of financial products. For example, when I led the brand research support for the merger of Bank of America and NationsBank in 1999, I used these tools to study 20 different lines of business, many of which operated domestically and others, globally.

Once banks began competing to become global integrated financial services providers—and quickly ran into trouble—I decided to combine the findings from those earlier assignments to see if I could figure out why these banks were having problems. I found that there was a wide range of brand attributes that affected the decision-making process for financial services (Exhibit 13.1). (Note: these were drivers of brand preference in the late-1990s, and they may be somewhat different today.) These drivers could all be categorized by two major factors: involvement and reassurance. That is, these two factors were almost always central to the decision-making process, at some level or another. Clients needed varying levels of involvement from the bank, and they needed varying levels of reassurance that they were making sound financial decisions.

If you group all the attributes in the above chart into the four quadrants shown, you can identify four distinct clusters: relationship, performance, access and scale (Exhibit 13.2). These four elements could represent potential positioning platforms for an integrated financial services provider.

When we look at individual products or services within the overall category of financial services, however, different patterns emerge. In investment banking,

Exhibit 13.1 Drivers of brand preference in financial services

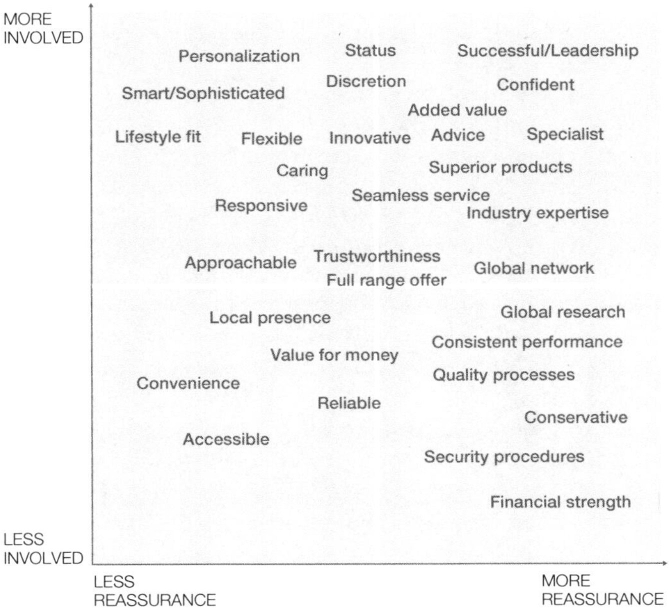

insurance companies as credible manufacturers of innovative or competitive investment products like mutual funds.

This finding raised troubling questions about the entire way the company was going to market. In response, the company completely revamped both its corporate nomenclature and its sales processes. Historically, life insurance agents were very entrepreneurial and self-sufficient. Their compensation came almost totally through sales commissions, and they rarely teamed up or referred clients to others. The fact-based research revealed that the individual agent needed to become more collaborative. He or she needed to be a true listener and determine what the client needed, and then bring in the resident experts to provide the appropriate products and services. Admitting that the agent didn't have all the answers—and that another representative of the company might be able to help—would actually increase his or her credibility in the eyes of customers.

But this change alone was not enough. If the selling agent was still presenting himself or herself as an agent from a life insurance company, the buyer was still likely to doubt that the company or the agent understood and could deliver superior investment products or advice.

Exhibit 13.6 Composite map of drivers of brand preference

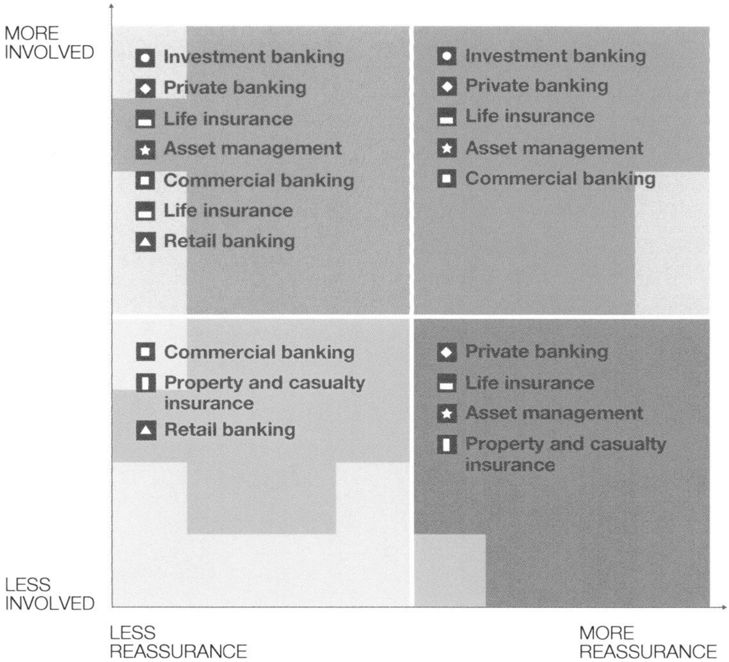

85

As a result, the company completely altered the way it went to market. "Life Insurance Company" was dropped from the branded name of the company (though it remained in its legal name). The distribution system became a financial network—note the implied collaboration—instead of a collection of life insurance agencies. The head of a local sales office is now called a managing partner instead of a general agent. The people who sell individual products are no longer called agents but rather financial representatives.

These changes proved to be more than window dressing. When the assignment was commissioned, this company was struggling to fill its quotas for agents. At college job fairs, prospective employees lined up to listen to the Wall Street firms instead. After the company revamped its approach, all that changed. Becoming a financial representative of a highly respected financial services firm—instead of an agent for a highly respected life insurance company—changed everything.

Summary
These two case studies demonstrate how conducting fact-based evaluations of the buying process in a "bottom-up" manner can provide valuable information that goes far beyond brand positioning, brand architecture and brand communications. Such evaluations provide insight into business strategy as well.

An ideal approach is to conduct such research for each line of business within your company, identify the key drivers of brand preference for each LOB and assess whether those attributes overlap with other LOBs. Substantial overlap in areas where your LOBs can credibly deliver provides a rich opportunity to build a powerful brand promise across the entire company. The key drivers that are unique to a particular LOB can be communicated at the LOB level (e.g., in brochures and other materials intended only for that LOB's target audience), while the overall brand provides support across multiple LOBs.

On the other hand, if your research turns up little overlap, it raises the question of whether building a strong corporate brand even makes sense. Perhaps the parent company should be a "house of brands" instead of a "branded house."

Of course, there are many other considerations that would affect the ultimate recommendation for brand architecture. Furthermore, if you find conflicting drivers—as with life insurance versus investment products or commercial banking versus investment banking—it might challenge the way you go to market.

Questions to discuss with your research professionals
+ Have we taken a bottom-up approach in building our brand promise?
+ Do we know the purchase drivers for our individual product or service brands, and how those brands are perceived by their key audiences?
+ Have we considered these factors in our brand architecture?
+ Is our strategy for going to market (e.g., product names, distribution names, brand architecture) appropriate to how people make choices?

Chapter 14
The Challenge of Missing Data

Because the tools described in Chapter 12 can be so powerful in adding value to your brand research, I think it's worthwhile to get "down into the details" a bit, to discuss some techniques that can help ensure that your data conforms with these modeling techniques. This chapter is intended to help your research professionals deal with the real-world situation of missing data. The first section deals with blank answers, or "item non-response," such as when a respondent omits a rating of one or more attributes. The second section deals with missing brands (i.e., when a respondent is familiar with more brands than the number you're asking him or her to rate).

I understand and appreciate that many CMOs and brand managers have limited interest in this level of detail and, because of that, I only summarize the topics here. If you'd like to read a more detailed discussion, please refer to *Fact-Based Branding in the Real World: A Simple Survival Guide for Research Professionals.*

An important caveat: the suggestions in this chapter are for calculating estimates for missing data primarily so that you can run advanced statistical analyses such as the models we talked about earlier. In contrast, the scores included in the various Brand Scorecards should only come from actual data provided by the respondents (that is, they should not include imputed values).

Imputing for missing attribute scores (item non-response)
If you're conducting basic brand tracking or customer satisfaction research and you don't plan to conduct any advanced analysis or modeling based on the data, you may not need to be concerned about missing data. You can simply ignore it and construct your means or score intervals—whichever you opt to use—based only on those respondents who actually provided a rating. On the other hand, if you're modeling the data to identify key drivers of preference or retention, conducting a segmentation analysis or other advanced techniques, it may be necessary—or at least advisable—to impute for missing observations.

> Most statistical procedures are built on the assumption that you have a complete data set (i.e., that every variable has a value for every record). In the world of survey research, this is rarely the case. Fortunately, there's a fairly simple yet highly accurate way of imputing missing values into individual records, which allows you to use standard statistical analysis techniques.

One way to avoid this problem is to require a respondent to answer every question. This may not be a good idea, however. I believe that most cases of item non-response, e.g., when a respondent rates a brand on most of the attributes but leaves one or more blank, are due to a lack of knowledge. Most likely, the respondent simply cannot provide a knowledgeable answer or does not have an opinion on it.

Suppose you ask an individual to rate a brand on a series of attributes, and one of those is "Service representatives address you by name." While the individual may be familiar with the brand, he or she may not have any direct experience with this aspect of the brand. The logical response is "I don't know." For purposes of modeling, a "don't know" response needs to be treated as a missing value.

So how do we handle such cases? The statistical literature is rich with suggestions for how to deal with missing data. Some say you should substitute the mean value or modal value from among the responses provided by others. Others suggest randomly selecting a value based on the distribution of the remaining responses. There are other ideas, yet none of these techniques is considered the "standard" approach for dealing with the problem.

In fact, there is no perfect solution. Statistical packages typically adopt one single approach as their default option, often leading to poor performance. A better solution is tailoring a specific approach that best aligns with the research currently being conducted. In *Fact-Based Branding in the Real World: A Simple Survival Guide for Research Professionals*, I examine a variety of techniques for imputing values for missing observations that lead to much better results than those often used as the default option in statistical packages. While they require a bit more effort to apply than simply plugging in the respondent mean, any decent researcher can program them quite easily using SAS or SPSS syntax or other programming techniques.

Imputing for missing brands

As we saw, micro-models that predict behavior at the individual respondent level are very powerful brand management tools. However, if a respondent is familiar with many different brands in the category being evaluated, this requires obtaining attribute ratings for each of those brands.

This can be quite difficult to do. If your model includes a large number of attributes—which it probably should if you're trying to fully understand buyer behavior—asking individuals to rate more than three brands can induce respondent fatigue. This can lead to "break-offs" (in which the respondent abandons the survey) or, even worse, situations in which respondents race to finish by providing nonsensical responses with little or no thought.

The first section talked about item non-response, or missing answers for individual attributes. At first thought, the concept of an entire missing brand seems far more challenging. How can you possibly predict with any accuracy how a particular person would rate an unrated brand on a series of attributes?

The first step is minimizing the occurrence of missing brand records. At least two things can be done in this regard. One is to **ask about as many brands as you can without inducing respondent fatigue.** While the threshold for respondent fatigue varies from respondent to respondent, I've found that most will rate three brands on up to 40 attributes. If you want to include a fourth brand, the number of attributes that can be used drops to around 20 or 25.

At least one leading research firm reduces respondent fatigue by asking respondents to simply tick the attributes that apply, rather than rating them on a broader scale. That is, the firm uses a binary scale (presence/absence) rather than a 10-point or other form of scale. One of this firm's statisticians has written a white paper documenting that this technique is as effective in identifying the key drivers of preference as the use of scales with more rating options or points. I haven't done independent research to confirm or discredit this assertion. However, I believe that this alternative is less than optimal since the world doesn't operate in a binary manner. This research methodology doesn't allow you to simulate improvements in a brand attribute, other than advancing from its absence to its presence. You can't evaluate having "more" of an attribute. For this reason, I don't recommend this method even if it reduces respondent fatigue or burden.

A second process that's useful both in minimizing brand non-response and in improving the predictive power of the resulting model is to **avoid asking about brands that the respondent is not familiar with.** As discussed earlier, if a buyer is not at least somewhat familiar with your brand, it's highly unlikely that he or she will choose it knowingly. So why attribute any share of preference to a brand with which a particular respondent is not familiar? In addition, if you do ask about such a brand, you'll likely get meaningless data for almost all the attributes about which you ask.

Nonetheless, even by limiting the brands in this way, there will be many environments in which the respondent is familiar with more than three brands. Consider consumer products such as cereals or soft drinks, for example, where you could probably name half a dozen or more brands off the top of your head. Hence, we still must confront the issue of what to do when we're missing data for entire brands.

One obvious solution would be to just use the mean ratings for the missing brand derived from others in the survey who actually rated it. This technique preserves the relationship between the various attributes within a brand, meaning that attributes for which those who rated the brand relatively high (or low) will have the same relationship preserved during the imputation process. But how accurate and reliable is such a procedure?

In fact, it's both accurate and reliable—surprisingly so. I conducted some research that examined the accuracy of alternative procedures for imputing for missing brands. I took an actual dataset from a survey in which respondents were asked to rate up to four brands they were familiar with, using a 10-point Likert scale. I then randomly deleted the responses for one of the rated brands for each respondent who had rated four brands, reducing the resulting database down to one in which no more than three brands had been rated—the protocol I recommend with large numbers of attributes. Different brands were deleted for different respondents. In all, about 15 percent of each brand's ratings were deleted through this process.

The results demonstrated that you can impute for missing brands with remarkable accuracy if you know the respondent's relationship with the missing brands (i.e., level of familiarity with and usage of the brands). At the "cost" of introducing a very small positive bias, which could be removed through subtraction, it greatly reduces the error variance and virtually eliminates outliers that could have a serious impact on the predictive power of the brand model.

The implication here is that if we can understand how decision makers rate three brands and their relationship with other brands with which they are familiar, we can estimate their perceptions of the unrated brands with remarkable accuracy—within 0.2 points on a 10-point scale.

Summary
Missing data comes with conducting research in the real world. But the presence of missing data does not have to keep you or your research professionals from taking advantage of some of the powerful analysis and modeling tools outlined in this book. That said, you shouldn't blindly accept the most simplistic or default methods for dealing with respondent omissions. There are reasonably easy methods for imputing for missing data with remarkable accuracy—within 0.2 points on a 10-point scale.

Questions to discuss with your research professionals
+ Do we allow respondents to respond "Don't know" to
   items, or to skip them if they're unable to rate them?
+ If so, how do we deal with the missing responses or
   "Don't know" answers for analysis purposes?
+ Are we simply using the statistical package's default option
   for imputations, or can we construct better estimates?
+ Are we obtaining brand ratings from decision makers who
   aren't sufficiently familiar with our brand? If so, why?
+ Are we asking survey respondents to rate too many brands on too many
   attributes? If so, we may be getting some data of questionable value.
+ What do we do when a respondent doesn't rate a brand with
   which they are familiar or provides so few attribute ratings
   that they may just as well have omitted the entire brand?

Compelling truth and brand management

This section discusses how you actually use the compelling truth of a brand to better manage brand strategy and messaging. It emphasizes the need to join art and science in telling better stories about brands. Other topics include a discussion of the employee as a critical audience of a brand, methods for displaying critical brand management metrics and using fact-based branding techniques to estimate the financial return on brand investments prior to implementing them.

Chapter 15
Compelling Truth and Optimal Brand Positioning

The discussion in Section 2 focused on identifying the compelling truth of a brand with fact-based research and modeling techniques. In this section, I discuss how CMOs and brand managers can use that information to actually manage a brand. This chapter looks at how you can use the compelling truth evaluation to detect the optimal positioning for a brand.

Why should a CMO or brand manager worry about a brand's positioning in the marketplace? Simple—if you don't manage how decision makers perceive your brand, the decision makers will manage it themselves. And you may not like how they do it!

The previous section of this book discussed the importance of identifying the most compelling attributes of a brand (i.e., those that matter to decision makers in a given environment) as well as how each brand in a competitive set stacks up on those key drivers of brand preference. Armed with this information, we can see how the various brands are positioned in the minds of the decision makers. In some cases, the perceptions of your brand may not agree at all with how you're attempting to position it in the market, at which point you'll probably want to re-evaluate your communication strategy.

A useful way to understand the competitive landscape is to map each brand's perceived performance on the most compelling brand attributes for that product or service. Many researchers prefer to map performance against the importance of key attributes (more specifically, against stated importance from survey respondents). I find the framework shown in Exhibit 15.1 to be more useful in mapping brand perceptions—it maps performance of the brand you're studying against the performance of brands deemed "best in class."

> If you don't manage how decision makers perceive your brand, the decision makers will manage it themselves. And you may not like how they do it! The compelling truth of a brand—the attributes that truly drive brand preference—provides the tools needed to optimally position a brand.

The vertical dimension of the chart represents the brand's mean score for the attribute (in this case, using a 10-point scale). This dimension answers the question, "Is the brand any good on this particular attribute?" I usually set the horizontal line in Exhibit 15.1 to coincide with the "average" score. In most environments, the "average" brand attribute score using a 10-point scale is around 7.0. (Recall that the typical range of responses for a 10-point scale is roughly 6.0 to 8.5.)

The horizontal dimension reflects the brand's mean attribute scores relative to the brand that had the highest score on that attribute (i.e., the best-in-class brand). Results in the darkened area to the right represent compelling attributes where customers perceive your brand to be stronger than any other in the competitive set—the areas where your brand is best in class. These are the true equities of the brand, and these attributes should be a central part of the brand's promise and messaging.

The upper left quadrant reflects strengths that you may not be able to use in articulating the brand promise the way you might like to. Even though your brand is strong in delivering those attributes, another brand in the competitive set is better—so much better, in fact, that decision makers would question the credibility of your brand claiming these attributes as equities.

A brand does not have to be best in class to highlight its strength on a given brand attribute. It does, however, have to be within a certain striking distance of the best-in-class brand. I've generally found that the acceptable "delta," or lag between the scores of the top performer and your brand, is between 0.3 and 0.5 points. Any more than that and you may not be credible in the market.

Exhibit 15.1 A framework for mapping brand perceptions

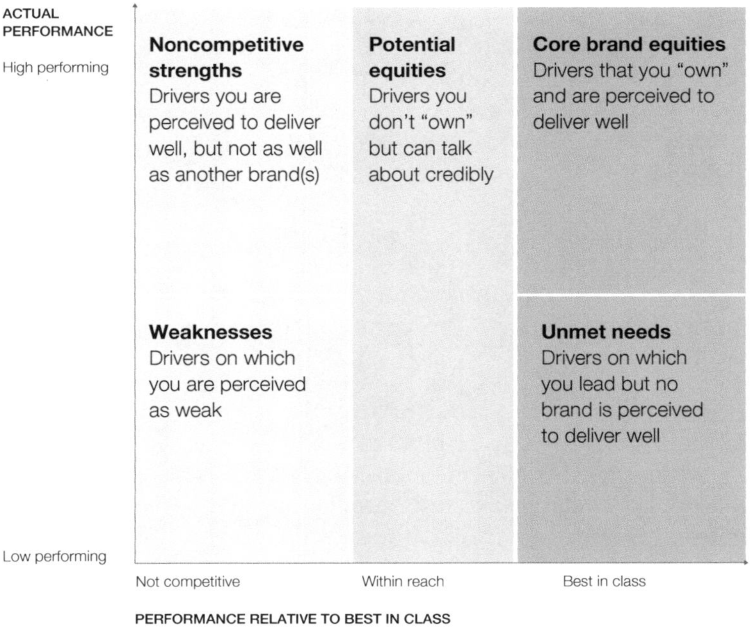

The lower right quadrant in Exhibit 15.1 is particularly interesting in that it deals with unmet customer needs. I've conducted numerous focus groups on unmet needs in various industries, and I've found again and again that consumers generally cannot describe their unmet needs. If you had asked people what they needed in 1900, they would have said a faster horse, not a car. The only attributes on this map are those that we've already determined to be compelling (i.e., attributes that will likely increase sales if you can improve them). Their mere presence on this map is proof that they represent a need among decision makers. And if the best-in-class brand gets a mean rating of no more than 6.0 to 6.5, it's clear that no brand is meeting their needs on that attribute.

Exhibit 15.2 is an example of a compelling truth or brand map for a brand in the two-way radio category. This map demonstrates that decision makers perceived the brand as the high-quality offering. Attributes in the upper-right quadrant—the brand's core equities—include aspects such as "superior audio quality," "advanced technology" and "rugged/durable products." So far, so good. On the other hand, another product is seen as being significantly

Exhibit 15.2 Example of a brand map

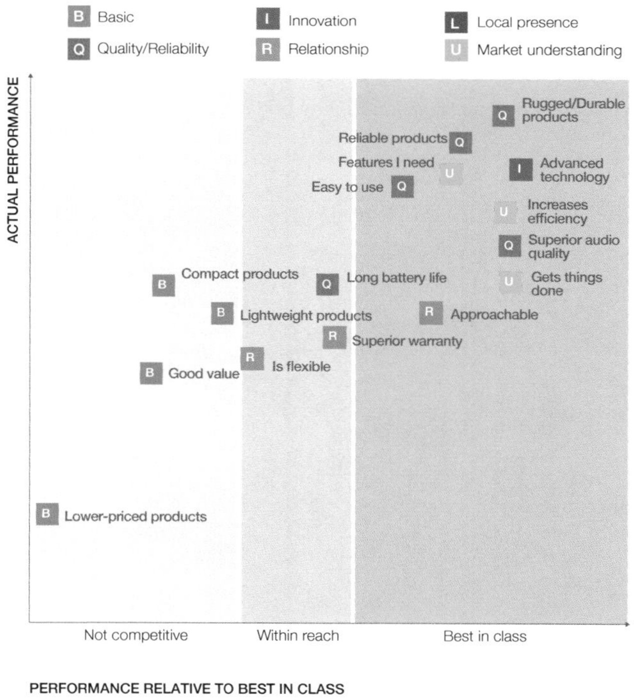

PERFORMANCE RELATIVE TO BEST IN CLASS

stronger in delivering a basic product for a reasonable price. How can you tell? Attributes in the left-hand quadrant, where the brand under study is not competitive, include aspects such as "good value" and "lower-priced products." When this manufacturer later acquired a manufacturer that was strong on the "basic" brand attributes, we recommended that it keep the existing brand—which was strongly associated with these basic attributes—rather than change the name and absorb it into the masterbrand. That way, the company could use the two brands to dominate both areas of the map.

Optimizing a brand's positioning

I referred to the "optimal" positioning of a brand in the title of this chapter. That was a deliberate choice. When you identify the compelling truth of your brand, you'll likely find that the more appropriate term should have been compelling truths, plural. This is because a set of even five or six brand attributes can usually be framed together to form two or three different brand promises.

How can you tell which one is best? The market simulator that we discussed in Chapter 12—the one that could predict the ROBI—can also be used to evaluate which of the alternative brand promises would yield the largest increase in brand preference (a surrogate measure for market share). However, that's not the only factor to consider. The cost of implementing and communicating a brand's promise and the company's culture should also factor into the selection of the brand promise you adopt. Chapter 19 has

Exhibit 15.3 Drivers of brand preference by business unit

The ideal brand promise would be some blend of attributes that benefit all three business units

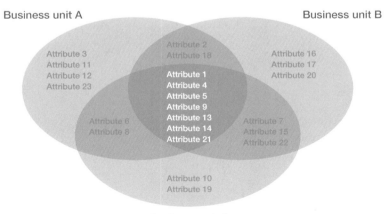

Business unit A

Business unit B

Attribute 3
Attribute 11
Attribute 12
Attribute 23

Attribute 2
Attribute 18

Attribute 16
Attribute 17
Attribute 20

Attribute 1
Attribute 4
Attribute 5
Attribute 9
Attribute 13
Attribute 14
Attribute 21

Attribute 6
Attribute 8

Attribute 7
Attribute 15
Attribute 22

Attribute 10
Attribute 19

Business unit C

a more detailed discussion of this, and it demonstrates that the brand promise that delivers the greatest share of market may not always represent the best return on brand investment.

Compelling truth and sub-brands (or "business unit" brands)

As the case studies in Chapter 13 pointed out—about the integrated financial services company and the life insurance brand—the methods in this book provide excellent tools for optimizing the brand promise for the parent company by first analyzing the compelling truth of the brand at the level of individual lines of business or business units. This "bottom-up" approach serves two purposes. First, it will identify the optimal positioning for the business unit itself. Second, by mapping the key drivers for each business unit and looking at areas where they overlap (Exhibit 15.3), you can identify those brand attributes that drive choice for more than one line of business.

In the example shown in Exhibit 15.3, the ideal brand promise for the parent brand would be some blend of the attributes that drive all three business units (i.e., Attributes 1, 4, 5, 9, 13, 14 and 21, as long as the brand is seen as credible in those areas). Attributes within a business unit's individual circle that don't overlap with any others then would be used as key messages in communications specifically for that unit (e.g., websites). That is, messaging at this level highlights only those attributes that drive brand preference for that specific product or service.

The dangerous allure of "the big idea" and "white space"

It's worth emphasizing here that branding and advertising serve different purposes. Branding strategy should remain effective for a long time, while advertising tends to be more temporal and campaign-driven. With the exception of remarkable advertising efforts like MasterCard's "priceless" campaign, advertising ideas come and go. In fact, many get passed around from one company to another within a category. How many airlines have run advertising campaigns around the themes of "up" and "rising"?

At the same time, many CMOs and brand managers often get the two confused, and this commonly shows up in branding campaigns that seek to capitalize on buzzword concepts like the "big idea" and "white space." While these ideas are occasionally relevant in branding, they're more appropriate in the advertising world. Apple continues to come up with big ideas for new technology products. It's what the company does, and consumers have come to expect it. Hence, this has essentially become Apple's brand positioning. But how many other firms or products come up with big ideas with any regularity? There are a few examples—Ugly Duckling Rent-a-Car and Rent-a-Wreck found some white space in the rental car market and certainly broke through the clutter—but one could question whether those proved to be successful brands. Brands are far more likely to be successful by understanding what their customers really want and delivering it better than anyone else in their competitive set.

I appreciate the need for advertisers to cut through the clutter. The world has so many ads, many of which are incredibly trite and/or annoying. Sometimes "annoying" is a ruse to break through the clutter, but more often it's just bad execution and a lack of understanding what consumers want.

> CMOs and brand managers frequently talk about their effort to find "The Big Idea" or "The White Space." Keep in mind that a lot of space is white because it's not a viable place to operate.

In relentlessly pursuing the big idea or trying to find the white space, CMOs and brand managers are searching for the branding equivalent of hitting a grand slam in the World Series. In reality, the brand that hits singles by executing consistently and understanding its customers' needs can generate a lot of business.

As mentioned earlier, I often use an 11-point, constant sum preference (CSP) exercise to determine a decision maker's preference for one brand versus another. Respondents get 11 "chips" to allocate between two brands in a head-to-head setting. When I look at the resulting distribution of chips for a given brand, it's striking how often a brand just barely wins or loses. In a significant number of cases, the chip allocation is six to five in favor of the brand, or five to six against it. It's like having the decision determined by a coin flip.

Exhibit 15.4 Distribution of chips received using an 11-point allocation

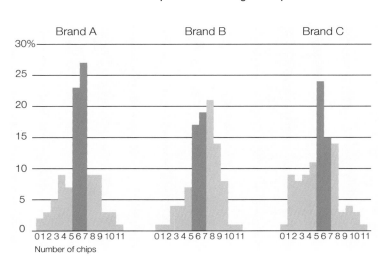

For example, look at the results from a recent examination of three brands in the scientific equipment industry (Exhibit 15.4). Brand A "wins" just over half of the time in head-to-head competitions, Brand B is a dominant brand that wins in 65 percent of the cases and Brand C is the mirror opposite—wins in only 39 percent of the cases. Yet in a remarkably high percent of the cases for each brand, preference was determined by a six-to-five or five-to-six margin. Think how easy it would be to tip the balance in this category by making even small improvements in the perception of a few key attributes. These are the equivalent of line-drive singles, not grand slams.

Summary

Effective brand management requires that you truly understand what customers want, you deliver on those needs and you keep your brand's messages focused clearly and consistently on both. Some brand managers look only at stated importance versus perceived performance, but these results can be misleading. A better approach is to map your perceived performance against the best-in-class brand for each attribute that drives brand preference. These results can help you focus your brand strategy and messaging around a credible story that matters. And if your company has multiple business units or lines of business, applying this approach in a bottom-up manner can identify the optimal positioning for each one as well as for the parent brand.

Finally, beware the allure of the big idea or white space. If you happen to discover a big idea, or find that customers really want something represented in the white space, that's great. But don't bet your brand on this approach. I appreciate the need to break through the clutter in brand communications, yet I also urge brand managers to keep in mind that a lot of space is white because it's not a viable place to operate. Using fact-based research to determine the compelling truth for your brand will take you a lot further than trying to swing for the fences on every pitch.

Questions to discuss with your research professionals

+ How did we establish our current brand positioning and brand strategy?
+ How are we presenting the performance of our brand?
+ Are we depicting brand performance against others in our competitive set?
+ How are we evaluating the viability of our brand's promise?
+ Do we have a way of simulating what would likely happen in the marketplace if we could change perceptions of our brand?
+ Do we understand the drivers of brand preference for our various lines of business or product/service brands?
+ To what extent is our corporate brand supporting the brand promise of our individual lines of business or product/service brands?

Chapter 16
Adding Art to Science: Storytelling and the Ethos of Simplicity

This book has focused almost entirely on the science of branding—fact-based techniques that can quantify key aspects of your brand. However, understanding the compelling truth and optimal positioning of the brand—and communicating those constructs—requires marrying that science with art.

Aristotle cited three principles of persuasion in his rhetorical theory (which we take seriously at Siegel+Gale, the company where I work):

+ *Logos*: logic and reason that's embedded in the language itself
+ *Pathos*: an emotional appeal directed toward the audience
+ *Ethos*: the character and credibility of the speaker

Sounds a lot like "compelling truth," doesn't it? This book has covered logos pretty thoroughly. But you can only achieve pathos if you convey your brand message in a way that strikes a chord with the audience.

> Communicating the compelling truth and optimal positioning of a brand requires both art and science. Ultimately, brand messaging is about storytelling, and most companies fail in this aspect because they aren't good storytellers. A key element of stories should be simplicity.

Ultimately, brand communication is about storytelling, but most companies fail in expressing their brand's value in the market because they aren't good storytellers. At Siegel+Gale, our researchers, strategists and designers join forces to identify the key elements of brand strategy, but when it comes to communicating the strategy and the brand's "voice," we rely on a team of professional writers (i.e., storytellers).

So why can't companies tell stories well? One reason is because they tend to spend most of their effort communicating what they do, rather than how their product or service offers value and benefit to its intended audience. That is, **they focus on the "what," rather than the "so what."** Manufacturing companies are particularly guilty of this. They love the products they develop (understandably) and they love to talk about those products. This is worthwhile, to a point—buyers need to know that a brand offers the item they're seeking. But the sale will ultimately go to the brand that truly convinces the buyer that the product will improve his or her life in some way—making his or her job easier, reducing stress and anxiety, making him or her look better on the job, etc.

It's not just manufacturers that fall into this trap. Other companies love to establish their scope of operations by talking about countable things, like the number of locations, assets under management, breadth of offerings and so on. While size sometimes matters, it's usually a threshold variable—beyond a certain point, it doesn't convince potential buyers that the brand is the best choice for them. Far more commonly, the key drivers of brand preference focus on how a brand will ensure success or peace of mind in some way.

The power of simplicity

Another reason that companies tend to be poor storytellers is that they make everything too complicated. This is where ethos comes into the equation. Companies need to **tell their stories within an ethos of simplicity**. People will never be persuaded by a message they can't understand, no matter how compelling and true that story may be.

In addition, simplicity enhances the credibility of the message in that simplicity engenders trust. As Irene Etzkorn, author of the book *Simple*, puts it, "Because simplicity allows no crevices in which duplicity can hide, the credibility of the source or ethos is more apparent."

Siegel+Gale was founded in 1969 as a document simplification company. In subsequent years, it expanded into a full-service global brand experience firm. Founder Alan Siegel abhorred complexity and instilled an appreciation of the value of simplicity that remains a core element of the firm's DNA to this day. Siegel+Gale uses the power of simplicity to help brands reach their true potential. Our goal is to help companies discover the essential truths of their organization, tell engaging stories that connect with their audiences and deliver meaningful experiences that are both unexpectedly fresh and remarkably clear.

Don't sell simplicity short. Simplicity isn't just nice to have; it could well be the next big differentiator in determining the companies or brands that succeed and those that fall short. The *Global Brand Simplicity Index* (GBSI) published annually by Siegel+Gale found that companies that establish simplicity as an integral part of their corporate ethos enjoy better business results. For example, consumers around the world indicated that they would pay an average premium of between 5.0 and 6.5 percent for simplified communications and experiences. In addition, the stock performance of the 10 "simplest" global brands widely outperformed major stock market indices (see Exhibit 25.1). As the world gets more complex, people crave simplicity, and brand promises that are built around this resonate with consumers.

An interesting case study in this regard is Southwest Airlines. Southwest's entire business model is built around simplicity. Its recent ad campaign focused on how it eliminates the red tape other airlines put in customers' way. The 2012 GBSI results show that non-customers rate Southwest as simpler to do business with than any other airline in the study—confirming that

Exhibit 16.1 Relative market performance

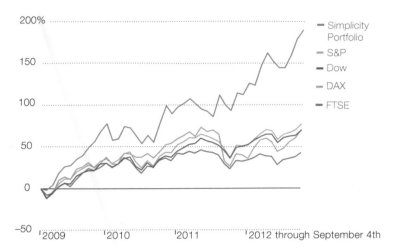

Southwest has raised the bar on passengers' expectations. But it also "walks the walk." Simplicity scores among customers exceed those of the other airlines by an even greater margin. In other words, Southwest sets higher expectations than almost any other airline and delivers on those expectations. No wonder Southwest's Net Promoter Score is almost off the top of the scale.

When Ken Segall wrote his book on Apple's success, he carefully chose the title, *Insanely Simple. The Obsession That Drives Apple's Success*. Quoting from Jonathan Ive, senior vice president of industrial design at Apple: "Simplicity isn't a visual style. It's not just minimalism or the absence of clutter. It involves digging through the depth of the complexity. To be truly simple, you have to go really deep. For example, to have no screws on something, you can end up having a product that is so convoluted and so complex. The better way to go about it is to go deeper with simplicity, to understand everything about it and how it's manufactured. You have to deeply understand the essence of a product in order to get rid of the parts that are not essential."

Six primary dimensions of simplicity

Simplicity does not mean simplistic. Even complex concepts can be told in ways that people can understand. So what does simplicity mean? Siegel+Gale evaluates simplicity across six primary dimensions:

+ Clarity: Can the message (meaning the communication, experience or other touch point) be understood without explanation?
+ Focus: Does the message reflect one clear strategic idea?
+ Freshness: Is the message original? Does it include an element of the unexpected?

+ Fit for purpose: Is the message relevant to the intended audience? Is it enduring? Can you implement it effectively?
+ Added value: Does every element of the message add clear value?
+ Relationship building: Does the message strengthen the relationship between the consumer and your brand?

Now that we've addressed the "art" element, let's go back to science once again. These dimensions can help you validate proposed brand promises or value propositions with key audiences. How? If you're testing alternative wordings (or "stories"), you can ask respondents to rate different messages on these dimensions, identifying the simplest and most effective messages. You can also use techniques like online bulletin boards to sharpen and simplify the language of the messages.

Summary
Building a strong brand requires a masterful combination of art and science. The science will help you identify the compelling truth of the brand, and art will help you tell the story well. If we go back to Aristotle's three elements of persuasion, perhaps the ideal application when it comes to branding is:
+ Logos: fact-based branding
+ Pathos: good storytelling
+ Ethos: simplicity

In other words, the successful and persuasive brand is one that can convey its compelling truth simply and consistently.

Chapter 17
Branding and Employee Engagement

So far I've focused the discussion of branding almost exclusively on external audiences—customers and prospects, investors and so on. However, a critical audience that many companies overlook is their own employees. These people are often the "face of the brand"—the bank teller or the department store clerk, for example—but they're also internal consumers. Companies that have a strong brand and a clear, simple brand promise are more likely to attract talented employees. They're also more likely to engage those employees in meaningful ways on the job each day, leading to a multitude of benefits.

Research companies in both the US and Europe have done considerable work to understand the nature of employee engagement. That research has identified two critical components:
+ How well does the employee understand the brand promise?
+ How committed is the employee to the brand promise as he or she understands it?

To assess brand engagement among its employees, a company usually asks them to rate both factors. Researchers typically use a 10-point scale, and they separate the top performers (i.e., employees that give themselves ratings of 9 or 10 on each factor) from everyone else. The results get sorted into a basic two-by-two matrix (Exhibit 17.1).

Obviously, you want as much of your workforce as possible to be in the upper right quadrant—those who both understand the brand's promise and are strongly committed to it. Some

In communicating their brand, many companies overlook their own employees. If you want your employees to be champions of your brand, they need to be engaged with it—they need to understand the brand's promise, and they need to be committed to that promise.

Exhibit 17.1 Employee Engagement Matrix

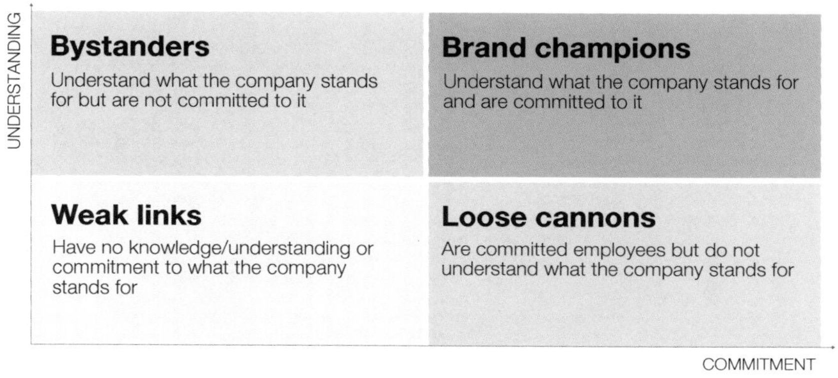

UNDERSTANDING

Bystanders
Understand what the company stands for but are not committed to it

Brand champions
Understand what the company stands for and are committed to it

Weak links
Have no knowledge/understanding or commitment to what the company stands for

Loose cannons
Are committed employees but do not understand what the company stands for

COMMITMENT

organizations refer to these employees as Brand Champions. Bystanders, who understand the brand promise but are not advocates for it, need to be motivated. But the greatest concerns are the Loose Cannons. This is a highly motivated segment of employees who are actively promoting something. Here, the goal for companies is to channel that energy and help them better understand the brand promise to make sure they're not offering rogue interpretations of what the company stands for.

Clearly, the Brand Champions in your organization do a better job of living your brand's promise and promoting the brand to customers. But if a company can successfully move more of its employees into this category, it will reap many other benefits. As shown in Exhibit 17.2—a real example from a leading manufacturing company—Brand Champions are more likely to use the brand, invest in the company's stock and give to the charities the organization endorses. In addition, strong engagement with the brand makes these people more likely to be satisfied employees, which reduces staff turnover and saves the company money.

What steps can a company take to create more Brand Champions in its workforce? The left-hand side of Exhibit 17.2 (the green and blue elements)

Exhibit 17.2 Employee Engagement Model

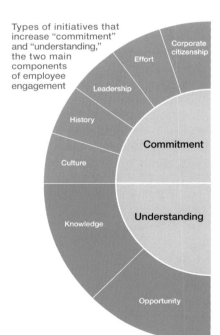

shows the types of initiatives that can increase understanding or commitment. For example, efforts that demonstrate management's commitment to the brand—both in what they say and how they act—contribute to the Leadership element that drives commitment. Environmental responsibility, philanthropy and other corporate initiatives contribute to the Corporate Citizenship component, which also drives employee commitment.

To gauge the current progress of your company in this area, you'll need to measure employee engagement. Analyzing the results by tenure, function and location can identify groups that need attention. (One caveat, when comparing locations, do not report results for a site or office that is so small that you risk compromising employee confidentiality.) Groups with above-average percentages of Bystanders are candidates for motivation initiatives, once you understand the root causes for their lack of commitment. For groups with higher than usual percentages of Loose Cannons, brand training programs are in order. If your organization has a large percentage of Weak Links across multiple groups, the organization likely has fundamental problems that go well beyond branding issues.

The percent of the workforce in the Brand Champion segment usually increases with tenure. There's something reassuring about that—familiarity breeds contentment, so to speak. However, this phenomenon is not always true. A recent measurement of employee engagement in a major technology company found the opposite trend, as shown in Exhibit 17.3. New employees were coming on board with great enthusiasm and commitment, yet a negative corporate culture was simply draining that enthusiasm over time.

Exhibit 17.3 Employee engagement and intent to stay, by tenure

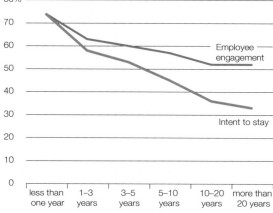

In addition, as employee engagement declined, employees' intent to stay with the company declined even further. These results caused great concern within the organization—with good reason—and the firm is working hard to rectify this situation.

Summary

Employee engagement—as indicated by their understanding of and commitment to the brand's promise—has serious implications for a company. Those employees who champion a brand deliver countless financial benefits, both internally and externally. On the other hand, committed employees who do not completely understand the brand can be dangerous. By measuring employee engagement and analyzing the results across different sub-groups (such as tenure, function or location), companies can find out which groups to prioritize and where to direct training programs.

Questions to discuss with your research professionals

+ What research do we conduct among employees?
+ Are we just measuring employee satisfaction, or do we measure employee engagement with the brand as well?
+ Do we have an employee engagement strategy, and is it aligned with our brand strategy?
+ Are we calculating an employee engagement index like the one described in this chapter? If so, at what levels do we report our results?
+ How are we determining what factors influence employee understanding and commitment?
+ Have we conducted any analyses to demonstrate the value of employee engagement to our company and/or brand?

Chapter 18
Tracking Critical Brand Metrics: the Brand Dashboard

An advantage of fact-based branding is that it generates results that brand managers and CMOs can organize into a Brand Dashboard to track key brand-related performance indicators. The dashboard gives a summary-level snapshot of the brand's current situation across multiple parameters. While you can customize the Brand Dashboard to the specific needs of your organization, I recommend using five principal categories of metrics: current business performance, brand positioning, social media performance, employee engagement and financial performance.

Business metrics

Business metrics should be available from internal sources. Examples of relevant business metrics include:

+ Sales by customer segment
+ Sales by geography
+ Sales by product
+ Sales by channel

> Fact-based branding generates results that CMOs and brand managers can organize into a Brand Dashboard to give them a summary-level snapshot of key brand-related performance indicators.

Brand metrics

A combination of market surveys and customer satisfaction surveys should uncover brand metrics. Examples of brand metrics you may want to include in a Brand Dashboard include:

+ Awareness (market metric)
+ Familiarity (market metric)
+ Usage (market metric)
+ Perceptions on key brand attributes (market metric)
+ Customer satisfaction (customer metric)
+ Customer loyalty (customer metric)
+ Likelihood to recommend/Net Promoter Score (customer metric)

Financial metrics

Financial metrics should be available from internal sources as well. Examples of financial metrics for inclusion in a Brand Dashboard include:

+ Revenue
+ Expenses
+ Profit
+ Market share
+ Price premium
+ Stock performance

Social media metrics
Social media performance has become a major topic of interest. In addition to the metrics examples shown below, I recommend constructing and tracking an "Influence Index" that measures the percent of those interacting with your brand socially that behave in a specified way (e.g., buy and/or recommend your product, etc.).

+ Social views
+ Referrals (i.e., traffic sources)
+ Share of voice
+ Connections (e.g., followers, fans, etc.)
+ Brand mentions
+ Customer experience
+ Brand sentiment (i.e., quality of engagement)
+ Influence Index

Employee metrics
Collected through internal surveys, relevant employee metrics include those related to:

+ Employee engagement
+ Employee satisfaction
+ Employee retention/attrition

Exhibit 18.1 shows a generic Brand Dashboard. Today, just about all enterprise software companies—from small boutique firms to giants such as SAP—offer some type of Brand Dashboard, with varying levels of complexity. The more sophisticated versions allow you to click on various statistics and view them in a multitude of ways (e.g., over time, by region, etc.).

Summary
Brand metrics merit the same level of attention as financial and business metrics, and they're just as fundamental to the business outcomes of the company. Brand Dashboards are a useful tool to help CMOs and brand managers track overall brand health and the effectiveness of specific brand initiatives. They can effectively synthesize the results of fact-based branding techniques into extremely useful, at-a-glance information.

Questions to discuss with your research professionals
+ If we already have a Brand Dashboard, are we tracking the right metrics? How can we make our Brand Dashboard more effective?
+ If we don't have a Brand Dashboard, what would it take to construct one? What are the most appropriate metrics for us to track on our Brand Dashboard?

Exhibit 18.1

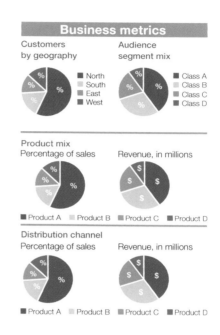

Brand metrics

Market	Q1	Q2	Pct chg
Awareness	%	%	%
Familiarity	%	%	%
Preference	%	%	%
Brand perceptions	%	%	%

Customer	Q1	Q2	Pct chg
Satisfaction	%	%	%
Loyalty	%	%	%
Willingness to recommend	%	%	%

Communications	Q1	Q2	Pct chg
Message association	%	%	%
Advertising awareness	%	%	%
Source of ad awareness	%	%	%

Business metrics

Customers by geography — North, South, East, West

Audience segment mix — Class A, Class B, Class C, Class D

Product mix
Percentage of sales — Revenue, in millions

Product A, Product B, Product C, Product D

Distribution channel
Percentage of sales — Revenue, in millions

Product A, Product B, Product C, Product D

Employee metrics

Understand brand promise — Committed to brand promise

Excellent, Good, Fair, Poor

Employee engagement index

Bystanders %	Champions %
Weak links %	Loose cannons %

Employee retention

Number of employees	Yr 1	Yr 2	Pct. chg.
	#	#	%

Financial metrics

Financial	Q1	Q2	Pct chg
Total revenue	$	$	%
Profit margin	$	$	%
Market share	%	%	%
Analyst ratings	AAA	AAA	—
Stock price	$	$	%

Social metrics

Social	Q1	Q2	Pct chg
Brand mentions	#	#	%
Share of voice	%	%	%
Brand sentiments	%	%	%
Influence index	#	#	%

Chapter 19
Estimating Return on Brand Investment

One of the biggest challenges that CMOs face is demonstrating the financial value of what they do. According to IBM's 2011 Global Chief Marketing Officer Study:

"Nearly two-thirds of CMOs think return on marketing investment will be the primary measure of their effectiveness by 2015. But proving that value is difficult. Even among the most successful enterprises, half of all CMOs feel insufficiently prepared to provide hard numbers."

It's far more difficult to build a predictive model for the impact of a branding initiative than it is for something like the introduction of a new product. Most CMOs don't have the tools that can determine the financial return on brand investments in advance of implementation. Instead, they often have to appeal to a CEO's conviction in the power of branding to get their budgets approved by advocating for the "try it and see" approach. However, fact-based branding techniques—like the market simulation model I described in Chapter 12—can predict the ROBI extremely well. Because this is such a powerful tool, it's worth discussing in more detail.

At a very simplistic level, calculating the ROBI for a brand initiative is a straightforward exercise, as Exhibit 19.1 shows. You measure a set of business indicators—such as revenues, sales success rates, profitability and so on—before you implement the brand initiatives. Then, sometime after the implementation, you measure those indicators again and attribute the change to the brand initiatives.

Unfortunately, this is a naïve model. The brand initiative is only one element that can affect these business indicators during the time between the two measurements. Other factors, for example, include economic changes and competitive activities (Exhibit 19.2).

Exhibit 19.1 A simplistic model for evaluating return on brand investment

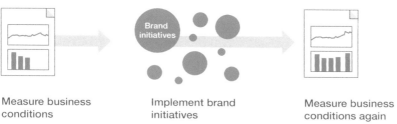

Measure business conditions

Implement brand initiatives

Measure business conditions again

Exhibit 19.2 Other forces affecting change in business conditions

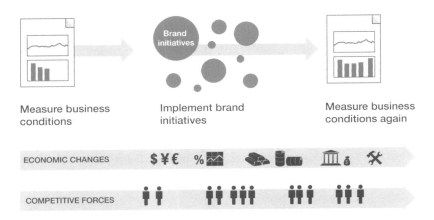

Measure business conditions

Implement brand initiatives

Measure business conditions again

However, we can address this by introducing an intervening variable—brand perceptions—into the model. The key is to measure decision makers' perceptions of the brand at both junctures—Time 1 and Time 2—along with the business conditions (Exhibit 19.3).

Why does this work? Brand perceptions are more clearly affected by reactions to brand initiatives than overall changes in economic conditions. During an economic slowdown, for example, people scale back their purchases, and they may not be buying your product. But if they still prefer your brand—and you

Exhibit 19.3 An improved model for predicting return on brand investment

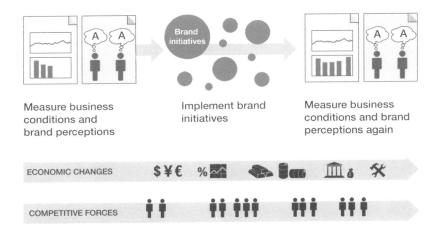

Measure business conditions and brand perceptions

Implement brand initiatives

Measure business conditions and brand perceptions again

launch an initiative that strengthens that preference—the initiative has succeeded and sales will increase when the economy comes back. Fundamentally, the simulation model explains the relationship between brand perceptions and share of preference (which is a surrogate for market share). The model includes changes in perceptions of the competitors' brands as well.

One challenge in applying this model is determining what initiatives to recommend and how much those initiatives can impact specific attributes in the model. The various Brand Scorecards can help immensely here. Those scorecards reveal how other brands are perceived, and some market intelligence will indicate the measures those brands took to achieve the perceptions they have. This enables you to make realistic estimates of how much the individual attributes will move in response to various initiatives.

In practice, you can only push individual attributes so far. Remember that we're modeling changes at this phase to predict their financial payoff. As much as you might want to, it's unrealistic to model a change of more than 0.5 points (based on a 10-point scale), over a one- to two-year period. Without some kind of dramatic event, such as an acquisition or other paradigm shift, changes of that magnitude are extremely rare. Simulated changes of 0.1 to 0.4 points for individual attributes are entirely plausible, however. They're the sweet spot for this model.

A quick note on the math: you calculate ROBI by dividing the incremental financial return resulting from brand investments by the cost of those investments. The simulation model gives you the numerator here—the incremental increase in revenue that you can expect as a result of the initiative. You need to multiply this amount by the margin or pre-tax profit on the incremental dollar of revenue for the brand's products or services. (The CFO can usually provide this for you.)

Calculating the denominator in the ROBI equation is straightforward—it's the total cost of each initiative. Make sure you factor in all costs, however. Will these initiatives require additional staff and/or training? Are you including specific costs to communicate and promote the initiatives? After all, if customers don't know about them, they won't have the desired effect.

Once you have both the numerator and denominator, the remaining task is a simple division.

A case study

Shortly before he left Halliburton, CEO Dick Cheney hired a branding firm to consult on Halliburton's brand. (Regardless of whether you agree with his political views, Dick Cheney is a very savvy businessman.) At the time, Halliburton was going to market under a variety of brands, including Halliburton Energy Services; Kellogg, Brown & Root; Brown & Root Energy

Services; and Landmark Graphics, among others. Part of the assignment was to determine if Halliburton could better leverage its corporate brand.

An evaluation of Halliburton's various lines of business, using the fact-based tools in this book, revealed that even though the businesses served very different functions, the purchasing process for them was remarkably similar. Buyers sought specialized expertise, proven results in maximizing the value of an asset and a company that was easy to do business with (among other key drivers).

These attributes suggested that the optimal positioning for Halliburton was around its people and processes. CEO Cheney disagreed, believing that perceptions of innovation were more important. He and others at the company were upset that Schlumberger, a competitor in the oil-services industry, had a reputation as the innovation leader, when Halliburton routinely won more awards in this area.

To determine which branding initiative would generate the greatest financial gains, the branding firm conducted an ROBI analysis of both strategies. That entailed designing two separate initiatives: one that would increase perceptions of the attributes related to people and processes, and a second that emphasized innovation-related attributes. After modeling them with respondents, we found that both approaches would have increased Halliburton's market share, however—to Cheney's credit—his approach led to a slightly higher increase.

However, the ROBI analysis demonstrated that this increased gain would come at a severe cost. Achieving Cheney's increase in share by emphasizing innovation would have actually lost money for the company—a lot of money. The ROBI for that initiative turned out to be minus 57 percent! In other words, the gains simply weren't worth the cost. In contrast, the approach that was recommended—emphasizing people and processes—yielded estimated ROBI levels of +43 percent in the first year and +70 percent in years two through five. That was the direction the company ultimately pursued.

Summary
Fact-based branding tools can inform brand positioning, brand architecture and brand messaging, but those are the things you'd expect these tools to do. The ability of fact-based research techniques to predict the ROBI of brand initiatives before they're implemented is truly a breakthrough. What CMO— or CEO or CFO, for that matter—would not jump at the chance to see such predictions prior to allocating capital for them?

There's also a secondary benefit: the very process of calculating the ROBI imposes a bit of order and structure to branding initiatives. For these models to work, the initiatives have to be well thought-out. You need to detail the attributes that you intend to change, along with the overall costs of implementing the initiatives (including communication costs). In all, this entire exercise—both the development of the models and the actual calculation of the ROBI itself—infuses an impressive level of due diligence into brand management.

Questions to discuss with your research professionals
+ How are we measuring the return on our brand investments?
+ Do we have any capability to predict ROBI in advance of implementation?
+ How can we develop this capability?

Customer experience research

The focus in this section shifts from customer acquisition to customer retention. It shows the relationship between customer experience and retention, and it suggests an approach for prioritizing various touch points to ensure that you're spending your customer experience improvement resources in the right places.

Chapter 20
Customer Experience and Touch Point Management

I've spent considerable time in this book talking about customer acquisition and how you can identify the compelling truth of your brand to increase brand preference. Once a prospect becomes a customer, however, success depends less on what you say about the brand and more on the actual customer experience you deliver.

This experience—positive and negative—gets reinforced through each and every customer touch point. By "touch point," I mean any circumstance in which the customer or prospect interacts with the brand. Touch points go well beyond the obvious things, like contact with a call center or a sales representative. In fact, touch points include the products/services themselves, websites, social media channels, letters, bills, brochures, instructions, physical environments (e.g., stores) and all other forms of customer contact.

> **The most difficult challenge in touch point management is identifying those touch points that have the greatest impact on the customer experience and retention. The customer experience is the composite of many touch point experiences. How do you separate the impact of each touch point, and what is the ROI from touch point investments?**

Any company that practices brand management and customer relationship management (CRM) understands the importance of touch points. They're the building blocks that form a customer's opinion of a company or brand. The challenge is in determining which ones really matter, and which ones are secondary. As with the acquisition attributes discussed in the last chapter, companies need to prioritize the touch points for investment and determine the ROI that might come from such investments. But how do you do that? And how do you assess the business risk associated with a specific touch point?

A couple of years ago, I spent a lot of time on this topic. A quick search on a popular search engine returned more than 2.5 million references for "touch point management." I read several of the articles, and almost all indicated that one of the first steps in touch point management is "to prioritize the touch points." No argument there. Yet I could not find a single article that provided a rigorous method for doing this.

Because there is so little guidance out there, in my experience companies tend to prioritize touch points in one of two ways:

1. In the informal approach, a group of individuals within the company

sits down and discusses recent customer satisfaction feedback (either through research or call center feedback). They prioritize touch points based on the "squeaky wheels"—i.e., those with the highest complaint levels.

2. In the more formal version, the company conducts a survey and asks customers to rate or rank the importance of various touch points as well as their satisfaction levels with each. The results get plotted on a grid. The "important" touch points where the company's performance lags importance are then given priority for improvement.

Neither approach is sufficient. The second method introduces at least a modicum of rigor, yet it's still not adequate. As pointed out earlier in this book, stated importance can be a very poor metric, since individuals often can't articulate how they make choices or how they allocate importance across various factors. Researchers continue to rely on this approach, but the answers just aren't valid. Some habits die hard.

So why is it difficult to prioritize touch points in a more rigorous way? As mentioned earlier, the overall customer experience is the aggregate of all the touch points he or she comes in contact with. This means that you can't simply survey customers who recently contacted your call center and determine the impact of that transaction on the overall customer experience. That's looking at just one brick, when you're trying to evaluate the entire building.

A second challenge is that the touch points are interrelated. Consider the following situation. An airline passenger arrives at the airport to fly to an important business meeting. She goes to the ticketing kiosk only to find that there's a problem with her ticket, requiring that she speak with a counter representative. The long line at the counter means she must wait 15 minutes. When she finally gets to the counter, the passenger learns that her ticket was improperly booked and must be reissued, taking more time. A lengthy wait in the security line, along with a gate that's far from the screening station, are the final hassles: she misses her flight and subsequently misses her business meeting. The woman contacts the customer service call center afterward to complain, but the damage is done.

So how should the airline (or the passenger) allocate blame for this customer-experience fiasco? Was it the kiosk interaction, the counter experience, the original ticketing agent, the security staff, the customer service call center she contacted at the end or all the above? The only element that didn't contribute to missing the flight was the call center, but if this passenger had been contacted in a transactional survey of recent callers to the call center—something most companies now do as a standard part of their customer-satisfaction research—it's likely the dissatisfaction would have appeared to be associated with the passenger's last point of contact.

There's one more complicating factor in prioritizing touch points. Clearly, the airline example shows that companies must measure the customer experience across multiple touch points for each customer in a survey. But that's an inconsistent base of comparison—different customers come in contact with different touch points. If you try to use traditional statistical analysis tools (such as regression), you have enormous amounts of missing data. Those holes exist because many respondents simply may not have experienced all touch points during the time period under study.

All in all, these issues make the problem very difficult. Two years ago, I developed a statistical tool called PinPoint™ that uses a creative method to get around these issues. (The detailed methodology is contained in *Fact-Based Branding in the Real World: A Simple Survival Guide for Research Professionals*.) Basically, PinPoint applies the experiences of other respondents with otherwise similar customer experiences to estimate what the touch point experience likely would have been for a respondent who didn't directly experience it him- or herself. That is, I found a way to estimate the level of satisfaction for each "missing" touch point that should have no impact on the overall customer experience. This allows the use of traditional analysis tools to allocate the impact across all touch points.

Once you've determined the impact of each touch point, it's relatively easy to construct a simulator that can predict the change in a customer experience metric such as the Net Promoter Score (NPS). This simulator can be used to predict the effects of individual service aspects within a touch point. For example, if you reduce the average wait time for customers who dial into your call center by 45 seconds, the model will tell you the effect of such a change on your overall customer satisfaction performance. This allows you to construct a dashboard for every touch point and every service aspect within a touch point.

Exhibit 20.1 shows an example of such a dashboard. It looks at a single touch point—pre-flight trip planning—and shows the impact that increasing the availability of flights to your desired destination would have on both passenger satisfaction with the pre-flight planning touch point and on the airline's Net Promoter Score.

Exhibit 20.1 Example of Customer Experience Dashboard

Touch Point Pre-flight planning
Aspect Availability of flights to your desired destination

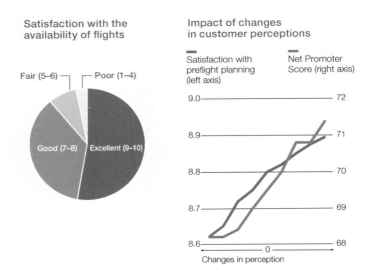

Satisfaction with the availability of flights

Impact of changes in customer perceptions

Satisfaction with preflight planning (left axis)

Net Promoter Score (right axis)

Fair (5–6) Poor (1–4)

Good (7–8) Excellent (9–10)

Changes in perception

Summary
Prioritizing touch points does not have to be an internal guessing game. In assessing a customer's experience with a brand and isolating the impact of specific touch points, you need to consider three factors:
+ Which touch points the customer experienced
+ The independent impact of each touch point on the customer's overall likelihood of recommending the brand
+ How satisfied the customer was with each touch point experience

While there may be other ways of parsing the impact of each touch point, PinPoint demonstrates that it can be done. Given the importance of the customer experience on overall brand performance, it's worth checking with your research professionals to see if they can help you with this important challenge.

Questions to discuss with your research professionals
+ Which touch points can significantly affect the overall customer experience?
+ How are we currently prioritizing the touch points to generate the biggest improvement in satisfaction for our investment?
+ Can we do this in a more rigorous manner?

Chapter 21
The Relationship Between Customer Experience and Retention

There seems to be a fundamental law in many companies regarding customer service: "If you have high customer satisfaction scores, you will not have attrition problems." This is the thinking that leads companies to invest hundreds of thousands of dollars on national or global customer satisfaction research and accompanying customer service improvements, only to find that they still have attrition problems. In fact, while customer **dissatisfaction** is a lead indicator of potential attrition, overall customer satisfaction is not the best measure of likely retention.

The problem is that many customers can be completely satisfied with the service they receive even as they depart. This is particularly the case with products or services that tend to be viewed as commodities. If customers do not see the value that a brand adds, they can be very happy with it and still jump on an offer that appears to provide the same product or service at a lower cost. It's pure economics.

> Customer dissatisfaction is a lead indicator of attrition risk, but customer satisfaction is not the best indicator of likely retention. Overall customer satisfaction is a great predictor of the likelihood to recommend a company, but the better measure of loyalty is the satisfaction that customers experience in relation to what they pay.

There's another problem with customer satisfaction as a retention metric: problems with the overall customer experience don't always lead to attrition. I repeatedly find that customers who've had a problem that the company thoroughly resolved are actually more satisfied overall than customers who never had a problem in the first place. This might lead one to speculate that a company could bump up its satisfaction ratings by giving all its customers problems and then resolving them well.

Even if a company were to consider this, however, only about one-third of customers typically let the company know they're having a problem. The rest silently suffer until they vote with their feet by leaving. My point here is that customers who do not encounter any problems or have any interactions with your company can come to believe that it offers no added value and that your product or service is essentially a commodity. These are the people who shop by price alone.

That's not to say that overall customer satisfaction is not a critical metric or that you shouldn't include it on a Brand Dashboard. In fact, it's a very strong

Exhibit 21.1 Likelihood to recommend a brand to others by overall satisfaction level

predictor of whether a customer would be likely to recommend your brand to others—the question upon which the well-known Net Promoter Score is based. Exhibit 21.1 represents a composite profile of five waves of customer satisfaction research in a business-to-business environment. The "product" is a business service that many customers view as essentially a commodity.

The exhibit shows the relationship between overall customer satisfaction and the likelihood to recommend the service to others. When a customer rates satisfaction with the service as a 9 or 10, there is a 99 percent likelihood that the customer would recommend the service to others. In 95 percent of the cases the service would get an unqualified recommendation. When the over-all satisfaction score drops to a 7 or 8, the likelihood of a recommendation remains high—95 percent—but in 13 percent of the cases people would recommend the service with reservations.

Once the score drops below a 7, undesirable outcomes begin to occur. The likelihood of an unqualified recommendation drops to 41 percent among those providing satisfaction ratings of 5 or 6, and there is a one-in-four chance of not getting a recommendation at all. With an overall satisfaction score of 1–4, there is only a one-in-three chance (37 percent) of getting any kind of recommendation.

The relationship between overall customer satisfaction and the likelihood to recommend the service to others is remarkably stable. Exhibit 21.2 shows the scores for each wave. Note how little the results vary by wave.

Exhibit 21.2 Likelihood to recommend a brand by overall satisfaction level, years one through five

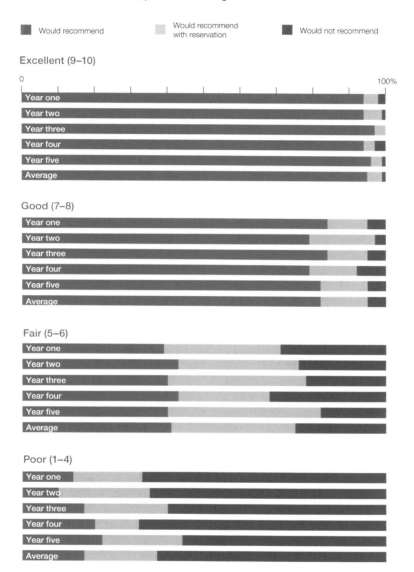

Exhibit 21.3 Overall satisfaction at time of attrition

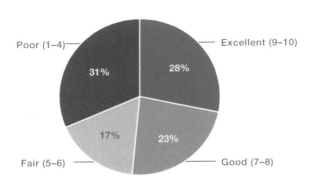

The relationship between perceived value and loyalty

While overall customer satisfaction is a very strong indicator of how likely your customers would be to recommend your product or service to others, it is less strong as an indicator of loyalty. A much better indicator is satisfaction with the value of your offering—whether people believe they are getting a fair deal for what they pay.

Exhibit 21.3 shows a profile of overall customer satisfaction among former customers at the time they left the service. (Note: these data are from the same environment as Exhibits 21.1 and 21.2 on the preceding pages.) As mentioned earlier, overall dissatisfaction is a pretty strong leading indicator of attrition and should be on the Brand Dashboard of every CMO and brand manager. Fully 31 percent of the customers who departed were dissatisfied with the service at the time they left (as represented by a rating of 1 to 4). This compares with only 7 percent of the current customers who rated the service as 1–4 during the same time frame. On one level, this seems intuitive—people who aren't happy with your product or service are less likely to stick around.

On the other hand, Exhibit 21.3 also shows that more than half of the customers (52 percent) rated their overall satisfaction as a 7 or higher, and over a quarter (28 percent) rated it a 9 or 10. These customers said they're happy, and yet they left.

Now let's examine the value parameter. Exhibit 21.4 shows satisfaction with the value of what they got compared to what they paid among customers who left the service. Suddenly, the overall number of satisfied customers drops markedly. Only 12 percent of the customers rated this metric as 9 or 10.

Of course, even satisfaction with value does not ensure loyalty, particularly for a business product or service like this one. Customers can stop using the service altogether, the decision can be overridden due to a merger or a new

Exhibit 21.4 Satisfaction with value at time of attrition

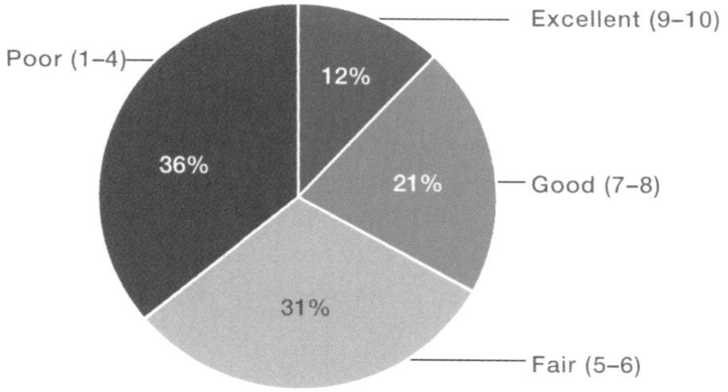

manager may make the purchasing decision, they can go out of business, etc. The point remains that brands should focus on satisfaction with value for the cost, not just customer satisfaction.

Summary
Measuring and managing customer satisfaction is an essential part of prudent brand management. However, overall satisfaction is a somewhat broad metric that doesn't always accurately indicate trouble spots. You need to measure other critical metrics among your customer base. The Net Promoter Score—based on customers' stated willingness to recommend the brand to others—is one such metric. Another is customers' satisfaction with the value they receive for the price they pay. This value metric is a much better predictor of potential attrition than overall customer satisfaction.

Questions to discuss with your research professionals
+ What metrics are we using to identify our at-risk customers?
+ Have we conducted any analyses that document the relationship between customer satisfaction (and other metrics) and actual customer attrition?
+ Are we measuring satisfaction with value for cost or just overall satisfaction?

Additional brand-related topics

This section looks at brand valuation and describes an alternative concept called "brand effect", which may be far more useful in evaluating the role brand plays in purchasing decisions. The section also explores customer segmentation modeling using brand preference (instead of typical segmentation approaches that rely on demographics or psychographics). Finally, the section describes a technique called Intent Translation, which allows you to correct for the difference between people's stated intentions in survey responses and their subsequent actions in the real world.

Chapter 22
Brand Valuation Versus Brand Effect

Each year, Interbrand announces its list of the Top 100 Brands, and each year it leads to a flurry of interest in brand valuation. In Europe it makes sense to focus on the financial value of a brand, since many European countries allow companies to list their brands on their balance sheets as corporate assets. In the United States, this is not the case. Nonetheless, companies like Interbrand and Millward Brown Optimor have built their businesses around estimating the dollar value of brands.

I've never understood the fascination with brand valuation. A CEO needs to demonstrate the value he or she brings to his or her company, but it seems to me there are better metrics for that than brand value. I think there's an ego component at work here—it's probably nice for an executive to brag that he or she is managing a company whose name and market perceptions are somehow considered to be worth more than those of other companies. Outside of that, however, I fail to understand why companies would pay extremely large amounts of money—usually $250,000 or more—to have a firm calculate a dollar value for something that can't even be cited on the balance sheet.

> Some companies pay large amounts of money to have a company conduct a valuation of their brand. But what do they do with the results? The brand can play a very important role in the purchase process, but how does a brand's valuation contribute to explaining how people make decisions? Answer: it doesn't.

Let me temper that comment somewhat. Brand valuation has a clear and defensible role in some situations. For example, it helps a company that is buying, selling or licensing a brand. Also, some companies use the brand's valuation as a benchmark for evaluating the effectiveness of their brand-building activities. If the value goes up from one time period to another, they must be doing something right.

What puzzles me is how to use these valuations in managing a brand. According to Interbrand, the Ford brand was worth $7.483 billion in 2011, while the Toyota brand was worth $27.764 billion. So how do I use that information in trying to manage the Ford brand? More specifically, how does that information impact the purchasing process among consumers (if it factors in at all)? Suppose you're in the market for an automobile and you've narrowed your consideration set down to two models—one manufactured by Ford and one manufactured by Toyota. Are you more likely to purchase a Toyota because it has a higher brand valuation? And what about pricing? Does the relative valuation of the two brands mean that you'd be willing to pay more for a comparable Toyota than a Ford?

Brand effect as an alternative to brand value

I'd like to describe an alternative metric for measuring the value of a brand in terms of how much the brand influences buying decisions—positively or negatively—rather than what some research firm thinks the dollar value of the brand is.

To understand the role of brand in a buying situation, let's walk through the process that people use to make buying decisions. To simplify things, suppose we're dealing with a buying environment in which there are only two brands—Brand A and Brand B. What elements would determine whether a buyer purchases Brand A? First of all, the buyer must have heard of Brand A and be at least somewhat familiar with its reputation if the brand is to have any influence whatsoever. Put another way, if the person is definitely going to make a purchase and is only familiar with Brand B, then Brand B wins. This has nothing to do with how good the buyer thinks Brand B is—he or she simply believes Brand B is the only option.

Now let's suppose the buyer is familiar with both Brand A and Brand B. In that case, the decision should depend on the buyer's perceptions of Brand A relative to Brand B. The buyer rates each brand on a kind of "subconscious scorecard," and the brand with the high score wins. Seems simple enough, but there's more involved.

As I've emphasized throughout this book, with the right fact-based metrics we can model the decision making process with a high degree of precision. Assuming that we've identified a good list of brand attributes and personality traits to include, the model will estimate the share of preference for each brand. In the years that I've been constructing such models, the results have been remarkably close to the actual market shares held by the various competitors.

Yet in many cases, when I examined the data more closely, I noticed a consistent difference between the share of preference that the model estimates and the share that's due to specific attributes in the model. My first thought was that this was just a normal sampling error or that I might have missed a key attribute or trait (or several) in the model. But a closer examination revealed a consistent bias in favor of the more powerful brand in the category. Additionally, the magnitude of the difference was larger in those categories or countries where the brand was more widely accepted as stronger. It became clear that there was a "brand effect" at work, something above and beyond the specific attributes of the product or service that also contributed to a brand's share of preference (and thus market share).

In short, it became clear that there are three main components that lead a person to choose Brand A or Brand B. First, as we just discussed, there's the awareness/familiarity differential that gives a well-known brand an automatic

22.1 Components of the share of preference

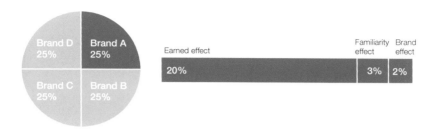

advantage over a lesser-known brand. We'll call this the **familiarity effect**. Second are the differences in perceptions between two brands among those familiar with both. We'll call this the **earned effect**, since it reflects the advantage that one brand earns over the other through its perceived performance. And the third component is the intangible **brand effect**.

Together, these three components add up to the share of preference, shown in Exhibit 22.1. (Note: Exhibit 22.1 examines the share of preference for Brand A versus Brand B.) As you can see, the brand effect becomes evident through the process of elimination. That is, the brand effect is the share of preference that accrues to one brand over a competitor **after differences in awareness, familiarity and perceived performance are removed**. It's the extent to which one brand is preferred over another simply through its reputation in the market.

From this definition, it's clear that brand effect is a relative concept—one that applies between two brands in a head-to-head competition—rather than an absolute concept (like brand value). Yet even as a relative factor, brand effect often has a big impact, and it's extremely hard for brands on the losing side of this equation to change it.

Note that the familiarity and brand effects for Brand A are opposite that for Brand B. For example, if the brand effect is +3.7 percentage points for Brand A versus Brand B, then it is −3.7 percentage points for Brand B versus Brand A. Additionally, in a buying environment that consists of more than two brands, Brand A's effect may be positive against one competitor and negative against another.

Brand effect versus the halo effect

Some readers might confuse brand effect with the so-called "halo effect." This is a concept that Phil Rosenzweig explains in his book, *The Halo Effect … and the Eight Other Business Delusions That Deceive Managers*. In fact, they're two different concepts. Rosenzweig uses the term halo effect to describe undue

22.2 Share of preference in a "two brand world"

The familiarity and brand effect "win it" for Brand A, regardless of Brand B's higher percentage of earned effect

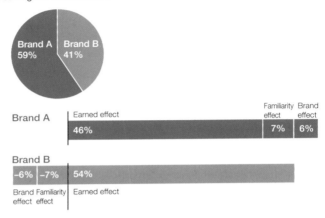

credit bestowed on successful companies or undue criticism bestowed on unsuccessful companies when trying to explain their success or failure.

Brand effect is much different. It represents a true, intangible brand-related influence in the purchase process. It basically quantifies the extent to which buyers are willing to purchase the product or service simply because it's from that brand. Recall the old maxim regarding corporate purchasing decisions: "You'll never lose your job if you go with IBM."

To better understand this concept of brand effect, let's go back to examining our old friends Brand A and Brand B. In the example shown in Exhibit 22.2, the share of preference for Brand A versus Brand (as derived from the CSP exercise among decision makers familiar with both brands) is 59.2 percent for Brand A and 40.8 percent for Brand B. However, among decision makers who are familiar with both brands, Brand B is actually the stronger brand based on the attributes in the model. Brand A enjoys a 5.7 point gain from greater familiarity and a 7.3 point share because of the intangible brand effect that it has built.

So what does this mean? It means that in a head-to-head competition with Brand B, Brand A has a head start of 7.3 percentage points before anything else is considered. You can put a dollar amount on that difference in this two-brand environment. If we combine the revenue for both companies, then the dollar value of Brand A in such a competition is 0.073 times the combined dollar amount. For a $1 billion product category, that equates to a brand effect of $73 million. To be clear, that's not the overall brand valuation (Interbrand and Millward Brown and all the others use their own methodology, which

22.3 Brand A's brand effect (relative to Brand B) by country

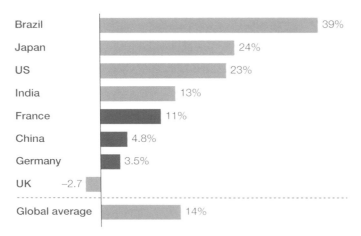

includes far more elements). Rather, it's the amount you can attribute solely to the intangible brand effect.

This has a significant impact on critical issues such as pricing as well. If your brand effect against a key competitor is negative, you may need to reduce your price (or increase perceptions of your brand) to offset this disadvantage. It's also worth including the brand effect in a company's Brand Dashboard. Tracking the brand effect will alert brand managers whether a leader is maintaining its lead or whether challengers are eroding that competitive advantage. It also tells competitors how much "better" they have to be—how much they need to improve their product or service offering—in order to level the playing field.

Consider the real-world example of two fierce global competitors in the technology field. Brand A enjoys a significant lead in the market worldwide, part of which is due to intangibles beyond pure performance. Brand B's management felt that it had all but leveled the playing field in Europe, however. Exhibit 22.3 shows the brand effect results using the methodology I described above. The results show that Brand B's management was correct. The brand effect that favored Brand A so strongly in the Americas and Asia was all but nonexistent in Europe. In fact, Brand B actually enjoyed a positive brand effect in the UK.

A final note before leaving this topic: the familiarity effect is an interesting component to examine as well. By multiplying the familiarity effect by the size of the market, we can monetize the potential gain that would result in increasing familiarity with a brand. In other words, this process of identifying the brand effect also produces a tool for estimating how much it would be worth to increase familiarity with your brand.

Summary
Virtually all CEOs now recognize the importance of their brands, and they routinely apply metrics to track the health of those brands. These are positive developments over the try-it-and-see approach of the past. That said, I wonder if brand valuation (i.e., the science used to assign a dollar value to a brand) is the most appropriate metric to apply. Apart from ego value, it's not clear to me why companies spend the money they do on brand valuation exercises unless they're about to buy, sell or license a brand.

A more useful exercise is to understand the company's brand effect relative to competitive brands. This information allows a CMO or brand manager to more strategically match up against specific competitors. If you know who your main challengers are, the brand effect lets you know how much of an advantage or disadvantage you have based on the brand's overall reputation, so you can price your product or service and communicate its strengths accordingly. Even in cases where you're competing against the entire market, e.g., a consumer product on a grocery shelf, understanding the brand effect against each competitor is powerful information to factor into your pricing decisions.

The calculation of brand effect requires you to determine the familiarity effect. This is an intermediate step, but it has value as well since it helps estimate the likely return from increasing awareness of and familiarity with a brand. This would help you predict the future value of such investments in advance. Equally important, it lets you estimate the effect a competitor's activities in this area will have on your brand.

Questions to discuss with your research professionals
+ If we've commissioned a brand valuation study in the past five years, what did we get out of this exercise besides a dollar figure?
+ How has the brand valuation study helped us manage our brand? Was it worth the expense?
+ How is our brand helping or hurting us when we compete against specific brands? Are our brands competing on a level playing field?
+ Have we conducted any analysis to determine our brand effect against specific competitors?

Chapter 23
Preference-Based Segmentation

Companies devote considerable effort in trying to identify distinct segments of customers and/or prospects. Frequently, these analyses look at things like demographic and "psychographic" (i.e., attitudinal) characteristics to define segments. Demographic aspects tend to be used more prevalently to help companies better direct their ad spending. Psychographic factors are particularly useful in developing messaging that will resonate with specific segments. That is, they help a company "play to the audience."

While these both have their purpose, there's a third option as well: a segmentation scheme based on brand preferences. This approach, which appears to be rarely used, allows us to analyze the decision process separately among those who prefer Brand X versus those who prefer Brand Y. Why do decision makers in the Brand X segment prefer that brand? Is it because they have different value structures—a separate set of criteria that they apply in making a brand decision? Or do they apply the same criteria and simply see Brand X differently than other consumers?

> Why do Coke drinkers prefer Coke and Pepsi drinkers prefer Pepsi? Do these two audiences use different criteria in choosing a favorite brand? Or do they use the same criteria and simply see the two brands differently? The answers to these questions have significant brand implications. Building separate decision models within segments based on brand preference can reveal the answers.

This is a critical question. The first situation—different value structures—would suggest that a company could offer sub-brands that would appeal to the different needs of the various segments. The latter situation—different perceptions of Brand X—would suggest an environment in which a single brand with a strong, relevant and consistent message is the ideal strategy (unless your brand is well back in the pack and has to resort to a niche strategy out of desperation).

If you don't know which situation you're in, you can't accurately position your brand in the market. That's why it's important to identify each segment of consumers for your product or service and model their decision-making process separately.

Segmentation in the rental car market
To demonstrate the value of constructing preference-based segments and modeling the decision-making process separately for each segment, I conducted an in-depth analysis of the rental car market. In particular, I looked

Exhibit 23.1 Key drivers of brand preference

+ Offers navigational features such as GPS
+ Rents cars that closely match the car I usually drive
+ Has locations near my home, office or repair shop

+ Is a brand for people who want to save money
+ Offers good value for the money
+ Offers the lowest rates

Common drivers
+ Is a brand I know and trust
+ Is a brand for business travelers
+ Is a brand for people in a hurry
+ Has fast, efficient check-in and return processes
+ Offers a wide ranges of makes and models
+ Rents clean, well-maintained vehicles
+ Rents vehicles that are brand new or have very low mileage
+ Rents vehicles with lots of room
+ Has convenient hours of operation
+ Makes it easy to make reservations
+ Has one toll-free number that connects me with any location
+ Is a brand for leisure travelers
+ Is a brand for everyday, regular people
+ Offers a superior membership/loyalty program
+ Rents vehicles with good gas mileage
+ Has professional and courteous agents
+ Offers rental vehicles both in-town and at the airports to which I travel

at a homogenous buying environment: individuals renting a car out-of-town (e.g., at an airport) for personal reasons and not for business. I examined three brands that generally appeal to people who travel out-of-town: Avis, Budget and Hertz.

First, let's examine how Hertz and Budget compete with each other. The initial question is whether those who prefer Hertz for out-of-town/personal rentals apply the same selection criteria as those who prefer Budget.

Modeling the decision-making process for each of the two preference-based segments—customers who prefer Hertz and customers who prefer Budget—using the principles discussed earlier in this book, we find that the two groups have 17 key drivers of brand preference in common (Exhibit 23.1). These aspects generally reflect the needs of the typical business traveler as well. It's all about the efficiency of the rental process and the quality of the vehicles themselves. (This is a considerably different profile from in-town rental decisions, where people typically choose a rental car brand based on factors such as convenience and pick-up options.)

Now let's look at the unique attributes that drive preference for each brand (shown under the respective logos in Exhibit 23.1). The three that were unique to Budget loyalists are critical—these renters are clearly very cost-sensitive. What's more, these three attributes were among the least important to Hertz loyalists.

What about performance on the individual attributes? On the three that were unique to Hertz loyalists, both consumer segments acknowledged Hertz's superiority (Exhibit 23.2). Both groups also recognized Hertz as being superior on the common attributes that both find important. Exhibit 23.3 shows a sample of the results for these attributes.

In contrast, for the two pure cost elements that were of unique importance to Budget loyalists, both segments acknowledged that Budget is superior (Exhibit 23.4). From these results, it's clear that Hertz and Budget are peacefully co-existing in the brand space, with Hertz delivering product and process excellence and Budget delivering needed services at a lower cost. (It will be interesting to see how this changes now that Hertz has acquired Dollar and Thrifty.)

Exhibit 23.2 Ratings for key drivers unique to Hertz loyalists

Exhibit 23.3 Ratings for key drivers common to both groups

Exhibit 23.4 Ratings for key drivers unique to Budget loyalists

Next, let's examine the two long-time rivals in this market, Avis and Hertz. Constructing the decision-making models for each loyalist segment, we find that they also share many preference attributes—mostly the same ones that Budget and Hertz shared (Exhibit 23.5). This reinforces the idea that almost all travelers renting out-of-town for personal reasons apply shared criteria.

On the other hand, there were some stark differences in the value structures of the two groups, which demonstrate the power of advertising. Hertz loyalists put more weight on a superior loyalty program (Hertz #1 Club Gold) and GPS (NeverLost) as well as other vehicle-related attributes. In contrast, Avis loyalists are more drawn to the human side of the business (e.g., employees who listen and understand, being treated as a valued customer, etc.). These may be due in part to the effectiveness of Avis's "We Try Harder" campaigns. (Ironically, Avis just announced that it is dropping this campaign after five decades!)

The two segments agree that Hertz is stronger in the area of offering vehicle features such as GPS, but in most of the 40 attributes the study looked at, Avis loyalists think Avis is best while Hertz loyalists think that Hertz is better. The people who prefer Avis ranked it as best in class on 34 of 40 attributes tested. Meanwhile, Hertz loyalists see Hertz as best in class on 30 attributes. That makes sense, right? As a further testament to the power of advertising, both groups see Enterprise as best in class on picking customers up—after all, the company's slogan is "We'll pick you up"—and on having locations closest to their home, office or repair shop. In addition, both see Thrifty and Budget as the best brands for people who want to save money.

Yet, look at the relative size of the leads for the "home team" (i.e., the preferred brand). The margin of victory for Hertz among its loyalists is much bigger than that for Avis among Avis loyalists. This is true for both the key attributes that are unique to Hertz loyalists and those that the two segments share (Exhibits 23.6 and 23.7).

On the critical attributes that were unique to Avis loyalists—the people and communication component—Avis loyalists believe that Avis is stronger than Hertz (Exhibit 23.8). However, even for those attributes, among Hertz loyalists Hertz was seen as stronger than Avis by an even greater margin. In fact, the only areas where Avis loyalists had larger leads related to cost (Exhibit 23.9). Recall that these are attributes "owned" by Budget or Thrifty, not Hertz or Avis. These results strongly suggest that Avis is seen as attempting to be a "Hertz wannabe" without a clear point of distinction.

This case study shows the value in segmenting populations based on brand preference. Hertz and Budget loyalists both view the two brands similarly, but they have critical differences in their value structures that explain why

Exhibit 23.5 Key drivers of brand preference

+ Offers navigational features such as GPS
+ Rents vehicles with good gas mileage
+ Rents cars that closely match the car I usually drive
+ Offers a superior membership/ loyalty program
+ Has locations near my home, office or repair shop
+ Has one toll-free number that connects me with any location

+ Has employees who listen to me and understand my needs
+ Treats me as a valued customer
+ Makes me feel like I made a smart choice
+ Is honest
+ Is knowledgeable
+ Is friendly

Common drivers
+ Is a brand I know and trust
+ Is a brand for business travelers
+ Is a brand for people in a hurry
+ Has fast, efficient check-in and return processes
+ Offers a wide ranges of makes and models
+ Rents clean, well-maintained vehicles
+ Rents vehicles that are brand new or have very low mileage
+ Rents vehicles with lots of room
+ Has convenient hours of operation
+ Makes it easy to make reservations
+ Has professional and courteous agents
+ Is a brand for leisure travelers
+ Is a brand for everyday, regular people
+ Offers rental vehicles both in-town and at the airports to which I travel

Exhibit 23.6 Ratings for key drivers unique to Hertz loyalists

Exhibit 23.7 Ratings for key drivers common to both groups

Exhibit 23.8 Ratings for key drivers unique to Avis loyalists

Exhibit 23.9 Attributes where Avis is stronger than Hertz

they prefer the brands they do. This results in Hertz and Budget living in peaceful harmony in the marketplace. There's a place for both, and both are understood.

In contrast, Hertz and Avis loyalists share mostly similar value structures but hold hugely different perceptions of the two brands. This means that both brands are fighting for the same customers and must, for the most part, "win" on the same attributes. Since the gaps in perceptions between the two brands are so much stronger for Hertz than they are for Avis, this puts Avis in a very tenuous position in the marketplace.

Summary

Many companies try to segment consumers based on demographics or psychographics, but a more useful approach may be segmentation based on brand preferences. This seems somewhat counter-intuitive, in that you're investigating the preferences of people who've already clearly indicated a preference. But the goal here is to determine why they prefer the brand they do.

Do they have different value structures and look for different attributes in choosing a brand? Or do they apply the same criteria and simply judge the brands differently? The answers have major implications in how you compete, and preference-based segmentation can help you determine those answers.

Questions to discuss with your research professionals

+ How are we segmenting our customers?
+ Have we ever conducted any research to determine if decision makers in different segments have different value structures? That is, do we know if different customers make decisions by considering different attributes?
+ Have we ever looked into preference-based segmentation?
+ Do we know how we're positioned in the minds of decision makers?
+ Is our position in their minds harmonious with other brands (like Budget with Hertz) or in conflict with other brands (like Avis with Hertz)?
+ If the latter is true, what are the implications on our marketing and communications strategy?

Chapter 24
Intent Translation: Developing Realistic Estimates of Action

A question that comes up all the time in brand and market research is: "How likely would you be to...?" In the case of new product research, the end of the question usually relates to the purchase of a new offering or configuration at a particular price. Companies want to know which product or specific features will have the greatest appeal and how much of that product is likely to sell.

In satisfaction research among current customers, the question may relate to the likelihood of continuing a relationship with the company or recommending it to others. In that situation, companies want to forecast how much of their current customer base will probably stay with the company and whether they might increase their spending on its products.

> Interpreting purchase intention data is difficult. It's one thing to say that you "definitely will purchase" a product when you're not being asked to put your money on the table, and another thing to actually do it. In fact, consumers behave much like an "object at rest." Unless there's sufficient motivation, they tend not to move.

Typically, the response options for such questions resemble those shown in Exhibit 24.1 (i.e., "Definitely would purchase," "Probably would purchase" and so on). But the difficult challenge here is not how to phrase the question or the responses; it's how to interpret the results. In the absence of a better technique, many researchers simply use the "top box" or "top two box" percentage as a surrogate measure for probable purchase (or renewal). Using the survey response data in Exhibit 24.1, this technique would yield probable purchase estimates of either 17.2 percent (top box method) or 41.4 percent (top two box method; 17.2 + 24.2 = 41.4).

Exhibit 24.1 Example of likelihood to purchase

Stated intention to purchase	Survey response
Definitely would	17.2%
Probably would	24.2%
Might or might mot	21.4%
Probably would not	21.9%
Definitely would not	15.3%
Total sample	41.4%*

* Top two box estimate

This is a pretty crude approach, however. There's no reason why the actual purchase percentage should resemble either of these two simplistic estimates. Not all of those who say they "definitely would" or "probably would" purchase a product will, in fact, purchase it. Some will and some won't.

Interpreting consumer intention data is difficult. It's one thing to say that you "definitely will purchase" a product as a hypothetical exercise and another thing to actually put your money on the table. In fact, consumers behave much like an "object at rest." Unless you apply a sufficient motivating force, most consumers tend not to move (i.e., take some action, like purchasing a new product). Reported intentions to change the status quo almost always overstate the amount of change that will actually take place.

Rather than using one of the "top box" techniques, a more realistic method of estimating the actual purchase percentage is to discount each response that indicates a change in the status quo. This is the principle behind a technique called "intent translation." As its name implies, intent translation discounts—or translates—a respondent's stated intention into a probability of action that more closely mirrors what would likely happen.

The technique is easy to apply (assuming 100 percent awareness in the marketplace, of course). For each response option that we offer, we need to estimate the proportion of people who give that answer that will actually carry out that intention—i.e., the percent who will actually walk the walk. This proportion is known as the translation coefficient.

For the response "definitely will purchase," for example, what proportion do we think will actually purchase the product if given the opportunity? It's likely to be far less than 100 percent. Unfortunately, there are few databases around that can be used to develop solid translation coefficients. Therefore, researchers typically apply "rule of thumb" estimates instead.

Exhibit 24.2 shows the set of intent translation coefficients that I've used many times in the past with reasonably good results. These adjustments have generated much more accurate intention results than taking the responses at face value or applying one of the top box methods. Applying the translation coefficients to the survey responses from Exhibit 24.1, we find that a more realistic estimate of the likely purchase (among those aware of the offer) is 15.0 percent. That's considerably less than the top two box estimate of 41.4 percent and even lower than the more conservative top box estimate of 17.2 percent. But experience shows it's a more accurate indication of future actions.

How does one determine the best coefficients to use? While the numbers above apply in general situations, the actual numbers will vary by industry, by product and by the amount of effort or discomfort that is involved in the actual purchase. For example, the coefficients may be quite high for a

Exhibit 24.2 Application of intent translation

Stated intention to purchase	Survey response	Translation coefficient	Adjusted estimate
Definitely would	17.2%	0.60	10.3%
Probably would	24.2%	0.15	3.6%
Might or might not	21.4%	0.05	1.1%
Probably would not	21.9%	0.00	0.0%
Definitely would not	15.3%	0.00	0.0%
Total sample	41.4%*	N/A	15.0%

*Top two box estimate

low-priced product in a category that everyone uses anyway (e.g., breakfast cereal). It's no big deal to try a new cereal, so the percentage of people who indicate in advance that they'll purchase it may be relatively close to the actual percentage in the market.

On the other hand, if adopting the product would require a significant action (e.g., changing a company's accounting software), the coefficients may be considerably lower. After all, this is a larger endeavor than switching from Cheerios to Lucky Charms, and the translation coefficients need to account for this. Even though you'd expect that respondents should have considered the cost of leaving their current relationship when they answered in the first place, that doesn't always happen. The product description may sound intriguing, leading a sizable proportion of the respondents to register intent, but the cost of exiting a current relationship—or the cost of the product or service itself—may be a significant deterrent to the actual purchase.

The best way to develop reasonable intent coefficients for your particular product or service is to build a database over time. By aggregating information from internal "case studies"—comparing pre-offering intentions from respondents and post-offering purchase levels after the introduction—you can gradually determine which coefficients are the most accurate. One way to do this is longitudinally by querying the same set of respondents before and after the product launch.

Of course, a survey that asks respondents their likelihood to purchase a new product or configuration automatically makes the respondent aware of that product. In reality, the individual may never have heard of the product prior to being surveyed, so you should apply the results only to the population of aware consumers, not the entire population. When developing a business plan for a new product, this means that you'll have to further discount the resulting purchase estimates to reflect the anticipated awareness based on advertising and promotion activities, product availability/distribution and other factors. So, if your marketing plan is likely to result in awareness of the new product among only 30 percent of potential buyers, you should assume 70 percent will not buy due to lack of awareness and apply the intent translation only to the remaining 30 percent.

A case study

In a major survey of life insurance policy owners, the sponsor asked respondents about their likelihood of renewing a particular type of coverage. In this case, the "object at rest"—or business as usual—is to continue buying the product. As shown in Exhibit 24.3, of those who reported that they "definitely will renew" their coverage, almost 92 percent actually did. This modest loss could be attributed to things such as rate increases, involuntary terminations of the policy by the insurer, death and other factors. Additionally, as I discussed in the earlier section on customer satisfaction research, many satisfied customers can be poached away by competitors if they don't think their current provider is offering sufficient value for the price.

On the other hand, 72 percent of those who said they "probably will not" renew actually did. That is, only **28 percent** ultimately acted on their stated intention of probably not renewing. Similarly, 26 percent of those who were definitely planning to leave renewed their policy, meaning that only **74 percent** who said they were going to leave actually did.

Note the similarity of these numbers—28 percent and 74 percent—to those used in the earlier "rule of thumb" example in Exhibit 24.2 (15 and 60 percent, respectively). These statistics reflect the fact that lapsing an existing policy in many cases involves a real cost to the policy owner above and beyond the inconvenience factor. Once again, it proves to be far easier (and perhaps less costly) to remain with the current coverage—the "object at rest"—than to take the intended action.

For the total sample, the longitudinal study—which used actual customer records to prove the action taken rather than re-surveying respondents—

Exhibit 24.3 Actual intent translation coefficients (life insurance renewal)

Stated intention to purchase	Survey response	Translation coefficient	Adjusted estimate
Definitely will renew	64%	0.917	58.6%
Probably will renew	33%	0.859	28.3%
Probably will not renew	2%	0.720	1.4%
Definitely will not renew	1%	0.257	0.2%
Total sample	97%*		88.5%

* Top two box estimate

found that 88.5 percent of the customers renewed coverage (Exhibit 24.3). This is lower than the 97 percent who reported that they definitely would renew (64 percent) or probably would renew (33 percent). If the company had not used intent translation coefficients to account for this difference, its forecast of future renewal would have been seriously flawed, in that it would have significantly overstated the likelihood of keeping its customers.

Summary

The purchasing actions of respondents are often substantially different from what they say they'll do in advance in response to a hypothetical survey question. Researchers who use a simple top box or top two box reporting convention don't take this phenomenon into account, and they're likely to overstate future purchasing action considerably. Intent translation is a simple process that restores credibility to these studies. It's easy to use and makes estimates of future action far more realistic.

Questions to discuss with your research professionals

+ Are we conducting research in which we ask a respondent's likelihood to take action?
+ If yes, how are we reporting that likelihood?
+ Have we ever conducted any research to validate our estimates of action against what actually happened?
+ Would intent translation be a useful tool for us to apply?

Afterword

Brand management requires many skills (and a decent amount of good luck as well). One of the skills that can give you a competitive advantage is the ability to use research effectively. Knowledge is power, and if you have more accurate information regarding your brand and its competitors, you can use that information to gain an edge in the market.

Specifically, fact-based branding principles can help your brand and your company succeed in many ways, by:

+ Identifying the key drivers of brand preference to ensure that you're focusing your brand messaging on relevant attributes
+ Identifying how customers and prospects perceive your brand and its competitors on those key drivers to ensure that your messaging is both credible and optimal (i.e., focusing on elements where you're competitive or have a clear advantage)
+ Simplifying your brand focus and brand messaging
+ Measuring and monitoring the customer experience with a focus on the touch points that are most critical in building customer loyalty
+ Estimating the ROBI before you implement major brand initiatives
+ Testing the simplicity and effectiveness of brand communications

To maximize your chances of success in the application of fact-based branding, I would offer three pieces of advice:

1. While it's probably impractical to develop hard-core expertise in brand research, at least learn enough about the topic to understand: (i) what research to commission; (ii) what questions to discuss with the research professionals who support you and (iii) how to recognize—or at least question—bad research when it lands on your desk.

2. If you don't have in-house research support, demand that the research and branding professionals who support you are seasoned and have at least a little bit of business sense. Unfortunately, companies spend a lot of money

hiring external firms to conduct research that's poorly designed and ultimately has little business impact.

3. If brand research, market research and customer satisfaction/customer experience research are not all under a single purview, build bridges to ensure that all these functions work together to capture a comprehensive understanding of the competitive environment in which your brand is operating.

Fact-based branding is not a magic wand. It requires a little more time to design the surveys and properly analyze the results, but it's well worth the effort. Over the course of my career, I've seen fact-based branding work for companies and organizations in virtually every industry around the world. I've seen companies in the food category use fact-based branding to determine how to position their brands and when and how to use private-label brands. I've seen major Fortune 50 companies adopt these tools as company standards to enhance their Six Sigma efforts. A major pharmaceutical company in Japan used the modeling techniques in this book to determine how it could extend its brand leadership in one category to a related category while minimizing cannibalization of its more profitable business. I worked with a health care system that improved its brand ratings a full point on a 10-point scale over three years, a level of improvement almost unheard of in any industry. This didn't require changing the company's operations—just a better understanding of its patients' preferences and a shift in how it communicated to those patients (and the general public).

As mentioned in this book, fact-based branding also led to the revamping of how life insurance companies now go to market. Understanding how consumers choose among credit unions, community banks and major money center banks reveals how each can differentiate itself and sustain a solid positioning in the financial services industry. I've even used fact-based branding to help some of the most well-known and highly respected not-for-profit organizations get donors to better understand who they are and help them stand out among the rising army of competing charitable organizations.

Adopting these tools doesn't require you to become a practicing statistician (even though it's hard to imagine a more exciting and fulfilling occupation). It just requires enough understanding to know good research from bad. Fact-based branding and the support of senior management are a winning combination. Good luck, and embrace the journey.

Index

micro-model 73–74, 76, 78, 90
Millward Brown Optimor 137, 140
missing data 11, 89–92, 127

N

NationsBank 70, 79
Net Promoter Score 37, 107, 113,
    127–128, 130, 133
Nissan 74
non-response 89–90

P

Paired Brand Scorecard 44–45, 48
Pepsi 13, 143
preference-based segmentation 13,
    143, 150
Prospect Brand Scorecard 44–46,
    48, 50

R

regression 73, 127
reliability 24–25, 53, 57–58, 82
Rent-a-Wreck 101
research:
  acquisition 10, 19, 20–21, 23, 27,
    30–31
  brand 4, 9–11, 13, 15–16, 19–20,
    23–24, 31, 37, 42–43, 48, 58,
    61, 63, 72, 75–76, 77–79, 89,
    157–158
  retention 10, 19, 20, 27, 31
Research International 32–33, 75
ROBI 8, 12, 74, 100, 117, 119–121, 157
Rolex 27
Rosenzweig, Phil 139

S

Saab 74, 76
Salomon Smith Barney 70
sampling error 53, 55–58, 138
SAP 27, 114
SAS 58, 90

scale:
  Likert 31, 33–34, 37, 39, 51, 92
  semantic 32–33, 39, 51
Schlumberger 120
Segall, Ken 107
segmentation 13, 89, 135, 143, 150
Siegel, Alan 106
Siegel+Gale 3–5, 105–107
simplicity 24, 105–108, 157
simulation model 13, 75, 117, 119
Six Sigma 4, 7, 158
SMART 32
social media 113–114, 125
Southwest Airlines 106
Spencer Stuart 4
SPSS 58, 90
Stated Importance
    10, 15, 21, 63–64, 97, 103, 126
statistical significance 53, 56–58
structural equations modeling
    (SEM) 76–77

T

Thrifty 145, 147
top box 34, 151–152, 155
top two box 34, 39, 40, 151–155
touch point 23, 28–30, 33, 107,
    125–128, 157
Toyota 74, 137

U

Ugly Duckling Rent-a-Car 101

V

variance 92
Visa 25
Volvo 74
VW 74, 76

W

white space 7, 12, 101–103